CHINA DURING THE CULTURAL REVOLUTION, 1966–1976

Recent Titles in
Bibliographies and Indexes in Asian Studies

Japan and the Japanese: A Bibliographic Guide to Reference Sources
Yasuko Makino and Mihoko Miki, compilers

Doctoral Dissertations on China and on Inner Asia, 1976–1990: An Annotated
Bibliography of Studies in Western Languages
*Frank Joseph Shulman, compiler and editor, with Patricia Polansky
and Anna Leon Shulman*

CHINA DURING THE CULTURAL REVOLUTION, 1966–1976

A Selected Bibliography of English Language Works

Compiled by
Tony H. Chang

DS
778.7
.C37x
1999
West

Bibliographies and Indexes in Asian Studies, Number 3

GREENWOOD PRESS
Westport, Connecticut • London

Library of Congress Cataloging-in-Publication Data

Chang, Tony H., 1951–
 China during the cultural revolution, 1966–1976 : a selected
bibliography of English language works / compiled by Tony H. Chang.
  p. cm.—(Bibliographies and indexes in Asian studies, ISSN
1086-5411 ; no. 3)
 Includes bibliographical references and index.
 ISBN 0–313–30905–1 (alk. paper)
 1. China—History—Cultural Revolution, 1966–1976—Bibliography.
2. English imprints. I. Title. II. Series.
Z3108.A5C37 1999
[DS778.7]
016.95105—dc21   98–44393

British Library Cataloguing in Publication Data is available.

Library of Congress Catalog Card Number: 98–44393
ISBN: 0–313–30905–1
ISSN: 1086-5411

First published in 1999

Greenwood Press, 88 Post Road West, Westport, CT 06881
An imprint of Greenwood Publishing Group, Inc.

Printed in the United States of America

The paper used in this book complies with the
Permanent Paper Standard issued by the National
Information Standards Organization (Z39.48–1984).

10 9 8 7 6 5 4 3 2 1

Contents

Preface

The Chinese Cultural Revolution (1966-1976), also called the Great Proletarian Cultural Revolution, was one of the most tumultuous periods in modern Chinese history. During this turbulent decade, many events happened in China: the Red Guards movement; the nationwide revolutionary rebels and great chaos; the fall of Liu Shaoqi, Deng Xiaoping and other party and state leaders; the military intervention; the forming of revolutionary committees to replace local party committees and administrative bodies; the Lin Biao affair; the movement to send millions of youth and intellectuals to countryside; the campaign to criticize Lin Biao and Confucius; the Tiananmen Square incident; and so on. It wounded many Chinese people in all strata deeply. During the different stages of the Cultural Revolution, millions of people were killed, committed suicide, or suffered unspeakable hardships both physically and psychologically.

The Cultural Revolution involved virtually all Chinese people and indirectly many other countries in the world. During the Cultural Revolution, revolutionary art, music, and dramas were pursued, and major reforms in education, factory management, economic planning, medical care, and other areas of Chinese life were carried out. Many of these actually brought bitterness and injury to the Chinese people. During this turbulent decade, China also encountered difficulties, setbacks, and isolation in the international relations area in the late 1960s, and made some efforts to improve relations with other countries and expand its diplomatic base in the 1970s.

Over the past three decades, studies of the Cultural Revolution have been well underway and thousands of works have been published in Chinese and in Western languages. Some works have given scholarly analyses and explanations of the Cultural Revolution. Many works have criticized, condemned, or praised the Cultural Revolution; many provided historical documents, reports, and accounts, explored detailed events in particular aspects, and recorded firsthand experiences. I am sure more documents will be uncovered and more works will be published in the near future, moving toward more comprehensive analyses and explanations of the Chinese Cultural Revolution.

To commemorate the 22nd anniversary of the end of the Cultural Revolution and the 32nd of its beginning, I prepared this bibliography as an aid for study and research on China during the period of 1966-1976, and as a guide to published English-language sources.

This bibliography includes selected books, monographs, theses, dissertations, and audio-visual materials in the English language that are commonly available to students and researchers. It includes works published up to the end of 1997 with a few forthcoming titles in 1998. While selecting titles, I consulted the Washington University Libraries catalog, the Harvard University Online Library Information System, the University of California's library catalog, the Library of Congress catalog, the OCLC online database, and other catalogs, online databases, and reference materials. The works were selected on the basis of their usefulness for information, study, and research. The selection varies from one section to another depending primarily upon the availability of sources. Certain out-of-date works are included in order to show the tremulous and intricate situation of the Cultural Revolution, and also show the disciplinary development of the fields. Publications in Chinese are not included in this bibliography. The scope of this bibliography is limited mostly to the period of 1966-1976, but a number of works dealing with subjects related to the origin of the Cultural Revolution and its aftermath are beyond that period. It should be emphasized that although they are not included in this bibliography, they are very important.

I hope this bibliography will be useful to the study and research on modern/contemporary China, especially the study and research on China during the Cultural Revolution period.

Tony H. Chang
St. Louis, September 1998

Introduction

This bibliography includes a selection of over 1,000 titles of books, monographs, theses, dissertations, and audio-visual materials. It covers a broad range of subjects related to the Chinese Cultural Revolution and its impact on China. This bibliography is arranged in eight main parts: Part I. Documents and Reference Works; Part II. General Works; Part III. Special Periods; Part IV. Cultural Revolution in Provinces and Municipalities; Part V. Special Subjects; Part VI. Biographies, Memoirs, and Firsthand Observations; Part. VII. Travelers' Reports; and Part VIII. Audio-visual and Microform Materials.

Part I is given over to Chinese Communist Party and government documents, Red Guards documents and publications, collective, selected historical bibliographies, directories, dictionaries, and other reference works. Part II, General Works, consists of works of a composite nature covering the entire period of the Chinese Cultural Revolution (1966-1976). Part III covers works which focus on four major periods: the great chaos period (1966-1969); the Lin Biao Affair (around 1970 to 1971), 1970-1976 (criticism of Lin Biao and Confucius, leadership succession crisis, elimination of the Gang of Four); and the trial of Lin Biao and the Gang of Four cliques. Part IV includes those materials related to the Cultural Revolution in provinces and municipalities. Part V is arranged according to various topics, such as military, education, culture, youth, women, intellectuals, religion, health care, population, science and technology, economics, law and legislation, foreign policies and foreign relations, social life, archaeology, art, language, literature, music, film, drama, and sports. Part VI is divided into two sections. The first section is a collection of biographies about major actors on the Chinese political scene as well as some ordinary people, while the second section consists of works recording the memories and firsthand observations of those who spent their lives living and suffering in the Cultural Revolution. Part VII contains travelers' reports. Many tourists visited China during the period of 1971-1976, and recorded what they were told and what they observed about Chinese life as well as the Chinese political system and social conditions. However, most outsiders at that time were restricted to visiting only certain "model" factories, communes, and institutions. Part VIII lists selected titles of audio-visual and microform materials.

The citation of works in this bibliography follows the form used in the original publication. Some personal names in the titles may cause confusion, because both the Wade-Giles and Pinyin romanization systems were used during different times (e.g. Mao Tse-tung and Mao Zedong; Lin Piao and Lin Biao; Chou En-lai and Zhou Enlai). In the author entries, if romanized personal names have been used in both Wade-Giles and Pinyin form, I chose to use the Pinyin form throughout the bibliography. For Chinese names written in traditional form, commas are not used after the surnames.

Each entry includes a full bibliographical description of the author, title, edition, imprint, and pagination. Brief annotations are appended to most entries to identify their special significance. Entries in main parts as well as within the subsections are generally arranged in alphabetical order. For works of single personal authorship, entry is under the author, compiler, or editor. For works of shared responsibility, entry is under a principal author, compiler, or editor. If personal authorship is unknown, diffuse, or cannot be determined, entry is under the title. All entries are numbered consecutively at the left margin.

At the end of this bibliography, three indexes of authors, titles, and subjects are provided. The alphabetical author index lists all authors, compilers, and editors. The title index lists all titles and selected subtitles in this bibliography and is also arranged in alphabetical order. Although the table of contents is arranged essentially according to various topics, users are advised to check the subject index for any topic that does not appear in the general table of contents.

CHINA DURING THE CULTURAL REVOLUTION, 1966–1976

I

Documents and Reference Works

A. DOCUMENTS

1. Asia Research Centre, comp. & ed. *Great cultural revolution in China.* Rutland, VT : C. E. Tuttle Co., 1968. 507 p.
   Contains a series of Chinese official documents dealing with the origins and development of the Cultural Revolution from 1963 to 1966. Includes a directory of key Chinese officials involved in the early stages of the Cultural Revolution, a glossary of the special political terms, slogans used in the Cultural Revolution, and a chronology of the major events from November 1965 to November 1966.
   Sequel: The Great power struggle in China.

2. Benton, Gregor, and Alan Hunter, eds. *Wild lily, prairie fire : China's road to democracy, Yan'an to Tian'anmen, 1942-1989.* Princeton, NJ : Princeton University Press, 1995. 361 p.
   A collection of sixty-eight documents divided into six categories: Yenan, 1942; Hundred Flowers, 1957; Cultural Revolution, 1966-1976; China Spring, 1979-1981; Prairie Fire, 1989; and Intellectuals' Critique, consisting of articles written after 1983.

3. *CCP documents of the Great Proletarian Cultural Revolution.* Hong Kong : Union Research Institute, 1969. 692 p.
   A compilation of 122 documents issued by Chinese Communist Party authorities, and 10 documents issued by the Beijing municipal authorities during the period of 1966-1967.

4.   Chi, Wen-shun, comp. *Readings in the Chinese Communist Cultural Revolution : a manual for students of the Chinese language.* Berkeley : University of California Press, 1971. 530 p.

Contains twenty-one documents which were selected from Chinese publications published during the period of 1965-1968. The first category is official documents dealing with the Cultural Revolution. The second is journal articles about the ideological conflicts among Chinese leaders.

5.   *Circular of the Central Committee of the Chinese Communist Party, May 16, 1966 : a great historic document.* Peking : Foreign Languages Press, 1967. 46 p.

6.   *Communiqué of the enlarged 12th plenary session of the Eighth Central Committee of the Communist Party of China (adopted on October 31, 1968).* Peking : Foreign Languages Press, 1968. 15 p.

Translation of: Zhong guo gong chan dang di 8 jie kuo da di 12 ci zhong yang wei yuan hui quan hui gong bao. Accompanied with an article: The revolutionary masses warmly cheer.

7.   *Communiqué of the second plenary session of the Ninth Central Committee of the Communist Party of China, September 6, 1970.* Peking : Foreign Languages Press, 1970. 14 p.

Communiqué of the Lushan Conference of 1970 which was a critical turning point of the Cultural Revolution.

8.   *Constitution of the Communist Party of China (adopted by the ninth National Congress of the Communist Party of China on April 14, 1969).* Peking : Foreign Languages Press, 1969. 38 p.

Translation of: Zhong guo gong chan dang zhang cheng.

Lin Biao was officially named as Mao's successor in this constitution.

9.   *Constitution of the People's Republic of China.* 1st ed. Peking : Foreign Languages Press, 1975. 61 p.

It was adopted by the National People's Congress on January 17, 1975.

10.   *Decision of the Central Committee of the Chinese Communist Party concerning the Great Proletarian Cultural Revolution (adopted on August 8, 1966).* Peking : Foreign Languages Press, 1966. 12 p.

Translation of: Zhong guo gong chan dang zhong yang wei yuan hui guan yu wu chan jie ji wen hua da ge ming ti jue ding.

It was issued on the 11th plenary session of the Eighth Central Committee of the Communist Party of China, known as the Sixteen Points (sixteen guiding principles of Cultural Revolution).

11. *Documents of Chinese Communist Party Central Committee, Sept. 1956-Apr. 1969*. Kowloon : Union Research Institute, 1971. 2 v.
A collection of documents issued under the name of Chinese Communist Party National Congress and Central Committee during the Party's 8th National Congress period (1956 to 1969).

12. *Documents of the first session of the fourth National People's Congress of the People's Republic of China*. 1st ed. Peking : Foreign Languages Press, 1975. 88 p.
Translation of: Zhong hua ren min gong he guo di 4 jie quan guo ren min dai biao da hui di 1 ci hui yi wen jie.

13. *Documents of the Ninth National Congress of the Communist Party of China*. Hong Kong : Hsinhua News Agency, 1969. 43 p.

14. *Documents of the Tenth National Congress of the Communist Party of China*. Peking : Foreign Languages Press, 1973. 98 p.

15. Fan, Kuang Huan.   *The Chinese Cultural Revolution : selected documents*. New York : Grove Press Inc., 1968. 320 p.
Documents selected for this collection come from Chinese official press publications covering the period of 1966-67. English translations of these documents are from Peking Review.

16. *Great power struggle in China*. Hong Kong : Asia Research Centre, 1969. 503 p.
A collection of official documents, radio broadcasts, and speeches by Chinese Communist Party leaders between 1967 and 1968, arranged under nine headings: The Red Guard movement; Spread of the revolution to the countryside and to industrial and mining enterprises; January Revolution; Nationwide struggle to seize power; Reverse in the power struggle; the Impact of the power struggle; the Army's role in Cultural Revolution; the Cultural Revolution in the army; the Problem involving the army.
A sequel to the book "Great cultural revolution in China."

17.   Hinton, Harold C., ed. *People's Republic of China, 1949-1979 : a documentary survey.* Wilmington, DE : Scholarly Resources, 1980. 5 v. (2,994 p.).
       Contains five volumes: v. 1. 1949-1957, From liberation to crisis. v. 2. 1957-1965, The Great Leap Forward and its aftermath. v. 3. 1965-1967, The Cultural Revolution, part I. v. 4. 1967-1969, The Cultural Revolution, Part II. v. 5. 1971-1979, After the Cultural Revolution.
       The editor provides introductory commentaries for each selection.

18.   *Important documents on the great proletarian cultural revolution in China.* Peking : Foreign Languages Press, 1970. 323 p.

19.   Kau, Michael Y. M., ed. *Lin Piao affair : power politics and military coup.* White Plains, NY : International Arts and Sciences Press, 1975. 591 p.
       Documents in this work are organized into five sections beginning with a comprehensive biography of Lin Biao. About one half of the materials are party documents, and the other half are from various Chinese newspapers and journals. It also includes comprehensive collections of Lin Biao's speeches, writings, and instructions from 1965 to 1970.

20.   Lieberthal, Kenneth, with James Tong and Sai-cheung Yeung. *Central documents and Politburo politics in China.* Ann Arbor : Center for Chinese Studies, University of Michigan, 1978. 201 p.
       Studies the Chinese decision making system by analyzing a particular stream of largely intrabureaucratic communications in the system-- Central documents. Appendix II lists all known central documents issued during 1966-1977.

21.   Lin Biao. *Report to the ninth National Congress of the Communist Party of China (delivered on April 1 and adopted on April 14, 1969).* Peking : Foreign Languages Press, 1969. 105 p.

22.   Lowy, George, ed. *Documents on contemporary China, 1949-1975 : a research collection.* Greenwich, CT : JAI Press, 1976-1977. 525 microfiches.
       Accompanied by a printed guide with same title.
       Contents include: Red Guard documents; Enactments of party and government documents; Research and analysis reports documents; Leadership information/bibliography/reference documents; Provincial/ municipal data documents.

23.   Lowy, George, ed. *Documents on contemporary China, 1949-1975 : selected research collection in microfiche*. Greenwich, CT : JAI Press, 1976. 2 v.
Contents: v. 1. Cultural revolution : Red Guard translations, bibliography, index / editor R. Sorich. v. 2. Bibliography, index for sections : bibliography/reference and leadership information / compiler E.B. Shera.

24.   Mao Zedong; Stuart R. Schram, ed. *Chairman Mao talks to the people : talks and letters : 1956-1971*. 1st American ed. New York : Pantheon Books, 1975. 352 p.
A collection of directives, statements, and speeches made by Mao Zedong during the period of 1956-1971, which includes Mao's talks with Zhang Chunqiao and Yao Wenyuan about January Revolution in 1967, and talks with provincial leaders about Lin Biao in August and September 1971.

25.   Milton, David, Nancy Milton, and Franz Schurmann, eds. *People's China : social experimentation, politics, entry onto the world scene, 1966 through 1972*. New York : Vintage Books, 1974. 673 p.
Materials were taken from scholars, journalists, literary authors and political leaders, including speeches and articles from Mao Zedong, Lin Biao, Zhou Enlai, Zhang Chunqiao, and Yao Wenyuan, as well as editorials from Renmin Ribao, Hongqi and other Chinese newspapers and magazines.

26.   Myers, James T., Jurgen Domes, and Erik von Groeling, eds. *Chinese politics : documents and analysis*. Columbia, SC : University of South Carolina Press, 1986-[1995]. 4 v. published.
A collection of documents covering Chinese politics from the start of the Cultural Revolution in 1966 to the early 1980s. Contents include: v. 1. Cultural revolution to 1969. v. 2. Ninth Party Congress (1969) to the death of Mao (1976). v. 3. The death of Mao (1976) to the fall of Hua Kuo-feng (1980). v. 4. The Fall of Hua Kuo-feng (1980) to the Twelfth Party Congress (1982).

27.   *Ninth National Congress of the Communist Party of China (documents)*. Peking : Foreign Languages Press, 1969. 175 p.
Translation of: Zhong guo gong chan dang di 9 ci quan guo dai biao da hui wen jian hui bian.

28.   *Press communiqués of the Secretariat of the Presidium of the Ninth National Congress of the Communist Party of China : April 1, 14 and*

24, 1969 ; Press communiqué of the first plenary session of the Ninth Central Committee of the Communist Party of China : April 28, 1969. Peking : Foreign Languages Press, 1969. 45 p.

29.   *Red Guard publications = Hung wei ping tzu liao.* Washington, DC : Center for Chinese Research Materials, Association of Research Libraries, 1975-1979. 20 v. (6,743 p.).
       Text in Chinese with preface in Chinese and English. Reprinted from various newspapers, documents, and other materials.

30.   *Red Guard publications. Supplement = Hung wei ping tzu liao. Hsu pien.* Washington, DC : Center for Chinese Research Materials, Association of Research Libraries, 1980. 16 v.
       Supplement 1 (v.1-8); supplement 2 (v.1-8).
       Text in Chinese with English preface. Reprinted from various newspapers, documents, and other materials.

31.   *Resolution on CPC history (1949-1981).* 1st ed. Beijing : Foreign Languages Press, 1981. 126 p.
       On cover: Authoritative assessment of Mao Zedong, the cultural revolution, achievement of the People's Republic.
       Contents include: 1. Resolution on certain questions in the history of our party since the founding of the People's Republic of China. 2. The Speech at the meeting in celebration of the anniversary of the 60th anniversary of the founding of the Chinese Communist Party--Hu Yao-bang. 3. Communiqué of the sixth plenary session of the 11th Central Committee of the CCP.

32.   *Resolution on CPC history (1949-1981).* 1st ed. Oxford ; New York : Pergamon Press, 1981. 126 p.

33.   Schoenhals, Michael.   *CCP central documents from the Cultural Revolution : index to an incomplete data base.* Stockholm : Center for Pacific Asia Studies at Stockholm University, 1993. 28 p.

34.   Schoenhals, Michael, ed. *China's Cultural Revolution, 1966-1969 : not a dinner party.* Armonk, NY : M.E. Sharpe, 1996. 400 p.
       Contains seventy-two primary documents mainly issued in the period of 1966-1969, which were selected from public and classified Chinese sources and translated into English.

35. Selden, Mark, with Patti Eggleston, eds. *People's Republic of China : a documentary history of revolutionary change*. New York : Monthly Review Press, 1979. 718 p.
Documents present a record of highlights of three decades of revolutionary change in China since 1949, including major laws and directives, Mao Zedong's writings, and other documents. Parts V and VI (p. 545-707) are devoted to the Cultural Revolution period.

36. Seybolt, Peter J., comp. *Revolutionary education in China : documents and commentary*. White Plains, NY : International Arts and Sciences Press, 1973. 408 p.
Materials translated were first published in the Chinese press. Five topics are discussed in the book: the broad objectives; conditions affecting educational theory and practice; the struggle between two lines; the events of the early years of Cultural Revolution; educational principles which were applied in 1970s.

37. *Tenth National Congress of the Communist Party of China : documents*. Peking : Foreign Languages Press, 1973. 98 p.
Translation of: Zhong guo gong chan dang di 10 ci quan guo dai biao da hui wen jian hui bian.

38. *Tenth National Congress of the Communist Party of China : documents*. Peking : China Reconstructs, 1973. 32 p.

B. REFERENCE WORKS

39. *Appearances and activities of leading Chinese Communist personalities*. Washington, DC : U.S. Central Intelligence Agency, [1968-1977?].
Provides a record of the known public appearances and activities of selected Chinese personalities. Arranged chronologically for each individual.
In 1971, title changed to: *Appearances and activities of leading personalities of the People's Republic of China.*

40. Bartke, Wolfgang. *Who's who in the People's Republic of China*. White Plains, NY : M.E. Sharpe, 1981. 729 p.
An alphabetical listing of individuals' biographies including national, central and provincial leaders as of 1980. The appendixes include historical records of the CCP Central Committee Politburo and provincial first secretaries, the ministers of the government, the

commanders of the military regions, and the ambassadors from 1949 to 1980.

41.   Blair, Patricia Wohlgemuth. *Development in the People's Republic of China, a selected bibliography.* Washington, DC : Overseas Development Council, 1976. 94 p.
A selection of books and articles on development strategy, economic and social performance, political and social conditions. Prepared for the China Round Table of the Washington Chapter of the Society for International Development.

42.   Central Intelligence Agency, U.S. *Bibliography of literature written in the People's Republic of China during the campaign to criticize Lin Piao and Confucius, July 1973-December 1974.* Washington, DC : Central Intelligence Agency, 1975. 220, 219 p.
A selective bibliography of English translations of articles which relate to this campaign. Contents include: Part 1. Alphabetical listing. Part 2. Chronological listing.

43.   Central Intelligence Agency, U.S. *Directory of officials of the People's Republic of China.* Washington, DC : Central Intelligence Agency, 1972-1977. 4 v.
An organizational handbook, also used for identifying the names and positions of officials. Covers party, government, academic, military and other Chinese organizations in domestic and foreign affairs.

44.   Cheng Jin, comp. *Chronology of the People's Republic of China, 1949-1984.* Beijing : Foreign Languages Press, 1986. 99 p.

45.   Cheng, Peter. *China.* Oxford, England ; Santa Barbara, CA : Clio Press, 1983. 390 p.
This bibliography presents a selection of over 1,450 works which provides basic information on China. Works cited are in English language, mainly published by American and British publishers between 1970 and 1982.

46.   Cheng, Peter. *Chronology of the People's Republic of China, from Oct. 1, 1949.* New York : Littlefield Adams & Co., 1972. 347 p.
Covers a day-to-day chronicle of events from 1949 through 1970.

47.   Cheng, Peter. *Chronology of the People's Republic of China, 1970-1979.* Metuchen, NJ : Scarecrow Press, 1986. 621 p.

Provides a day-to-day chronicle of events during the 1970's, which is a supplement to the author's "Chronology of the Peoples Republic of China, from Oct. 1, 1949."

48.   Cheng, Peter. *Current books on China, 1983-1988 : an annotated bibliography*. New York ; London : Garland Publishing, 1990. 268 p.
Over 500 works cited are in English, and published mainly by American or British publishers between 1983 and 1988.

49.   *Chinese Communist who's who*. Taipei : Institute of International Relations, 1970-1971. 2 v.
An updated English edition of "Zhong gong ren ming lu."

50.   *Cultural Revolution : a sourcebook for Foreign Cultures 48, Spring 1997--Professor R. MacFarquhar*. Cambridge, MA : Harvard University, 1997. 2 v.

51.   Emerson, John Philip et al. *Provinces of the People's Republic of China : a political and economic bibliography*. Washington, DC : U.S. Department of Commerce, Bureau of Economic Analysis, 1976. 734 p.
A bibliographical work containing over 6,000 citations of source of data and information on the political and economic developments at the provincial level in China.

52.   Fraser, Stewart E. and Kuang-liang Hsu. *China--the Cultural Revolution, its aftermath and effects on education and society : a select and partially annotated bibliography*. London : University of London, Institute of Education, 1972. 102 p.

53.   Fraser, Stewart E. and Kuang-liang Hsu. *Chinese education and society : a bibliographic guide : the cultural revolution and its aftermath*. White Plains, NY : International Arts and Sciences Press, 1972. 204 p.
A bibliographic guide on Chinese education including subjects of primary and secondary education, teacher training, higher education, agricultural education, international relations education, educational development. Sources are mainly English and Chinese language publications with some in Japanese, French, German and other languages.

54.   Geelan, P. J. M. and D. C. Twitchett, eds. *Times atlas of China*. London : Times Books, 1974. 145, 27 p.

Includes historical, economic, thematic, and physical maps, also includes provincial maps and city plans.

55.   *Glossary of Chinese communist terms and phrases*. Revised ed. Washington, DC ; Springfield, VA : Joint Publications Research Service, 1969. 113 p.
Text in English and Chinese.

56.   *Glossary of Chinese communist terms and phrases used during the Cultural Revolution*. [S.l. : s.n], 1968. 26 leaves.
Documentation on specific topics are taken mainly from the presses and radio stations in China.

57.   Goehlert, Robert. *The Chinese cultural revolution : a selected bibliography*. Monticello, IL : Vance Bibliographies, 1988. 10 p.

58.   Goodman, David S. G. *China's provincial leaders, 1949-1985*. Atlantic Highlands, NJ : Humanities Press International, 1986-1987. 3 v.
Identifies individuals and their positions held by provincial and regional level unit, from 1949 till 1985.
Vol. 1 is a directory identifying the leaders by province or region. Vols. 2 and 3 provide detailed biographies.

59.   Goodman, David S. G. *Research guide to Chinese provincial and regional newspapers*. London : Contemporary China Institute, School of Oriental and African Studies, University of London, 1976. 140 p.

60.   Gordon, Leonard H. D. and Frank J. Shulman, comps. & eds. *Doctoral dissertations on China : a bibliography of studies in Western languages, 1945-1970*. Seattle : Published for the Association for Asian Studies by the University of Washington Press, 1972. 317 p.

61.   Gregory, Peter B. and Noele Krenkel. *China : education since the Cultural Revolution : selected, partially annotated bibliography of English translations*. San Francisco : Evaluation and Research Analysts, 1972. 1 v.

62.   Kaplan, Fredric M., Julian M. Sobin, and Stephen Andors, eds. *Encyclopedia of China today*. 1st ed. Fair Lawn, NJ : Eurasia Press ; New York : distributed in the U.S. by Harper & Row, 1979. 336 p.

A comprehensible overview of China, covering most of the important aspects of China's development in the 1970s. Much of the information contained was derived from materials developed in China.

63. Lamb, Malcolm. *Directory of Chinese officials and organizations, 1968-1978*. Revised ed. Canberra : Contemporary China Centre, Research School of Pacific Studies, Australian National University, 1978. 285 p.
Cover title: Directory of officials in the People's Republic of China, 1968-1978.
Previous edition was published in 1976 under the title: *Directory of Central official in the People's Republic of China, 1968-1975.*

64. Lamb, Malcolm. *Directory of officials and organizations in China, 1968-1983*. Armonk, NY : M.E. Sharpe, 1984. 717 p.
An updated edition.

65. Lau, Yee-fui, Ho Wan-yee, and Yeung Sai-cheung, eds. *Glossary of Chinese political phrases*. Hong Kong : Union Research Institute, 1977. 590 p.
Contains over 2,070 entries.

66. Lee, Hong Yung. *A research guide to Red Guard publications, 1966-1969*. Armonk, NY : M.E. Sharpe, 1989. 289 p.
Provides comprehensive information on the thousands of Red Guard publications published during the period of 1966-1969.

67. Leung, Edwin Pak-wah, ed. *Historical dictionary of revolutionary China, 1839-1976*. New York : Greenwood Press, 1992. 566 p.
Covers events, ideas, personalities, battles, organizations and other topics for the entire period between 1839 and 1976. The appended chronology provides an overview of the Chinese revolutionary movements.

68. Li Ku-cheng. *Glossary of political terms of the People's Republic of China*. Hong Kong : Chinese University Press, c1995. 639 p.
A collection of 560 important and frequently-used Chinese political terms and phrases that appeared between 1949 and 1990. Each entry begins with an explanation of the term and its origin, a description of how and under what circumstances the term was used, and a discussion of the change of meaning over the years, as well as the political and

social significance of the words. Terms and indexes in English and Chinese, definitions in English.
Translation of: Zhong guo da lu zheng zhi shu yu.

69.   Lieberthal, Kenneth. *A research guide to central party and government meetings in China, 1949-1975*. White Plains, NY : International Arts and Sciences Press, c1976. 322 p.
Specifies the documentary information available on meetings and gatherings of the Chinese Communist Party Politburo, Standing Committee of the Politburo, Military Affairs Committee, Central Cultural Revolution Group, Central Committee Plenums, PLA political work conferences, National People's Congress, and others.

70.   Lieberthal, Kenneth and Bruce J. Dickson. *A research guide to central party and government meetings in China, 1949-1986*. Revised and expanded ed. Armonk, NY : M.E. Sharpe, c1989. 339 p.
Spine title: *A research guide to central meetings in China*.

71.   Lu Hsun Library, Prague, comp. *List of Red Guard publications in the Lu Hsun Library of the Oriental Institute, Prague*. Prague : Oriental Institute in Academia, Publishing House of the Czechoslovak Academy of Sciences, 1975. 145 p.
A list of 225 Red Guard newspaper and periodical titles in 577 issues, mostly published in China between 1966 and 1968.

72.   Party History Research Centre. *History of the Chinese Communist Party : a chronology of events, 1919-1990*. 1st ed. Beijing : Foreign Languages Press, 1991. 524 p.
Compiled by the Party History Research Centre of the Central Committee of the Chinese Communist Party. Contents include: VIII. The period of the Cultural Revolution, May 1966-Oct. 1976 (p. 323-378).

73.   Scalapino, Robert A., ed. *Elites in the People's Republic of China*. Seattle : University of Washington Press, 1972. 671 p.
Consists of a collection of essays studying on the Chinese communist political leaders at the national level, military leaders and provincial leaders.

74.   Shulman, Frank, comp. & ed. *Doctoral dissertations on China, 1971-1975 : a bibliography of studies in Western languages*. Seattle : University of Washington Press, 1978. 329 p.

75. State Statistical Bureau, PRC. *China statistical yearbook, 1989.* New York : Praeger Publishers, 1990. 840 p.
     An English translation and revision of the official China Statistical Yearbook. It has about 1,000 statistical tables containing national and provincial data in social and economic fields for the year 1988, as well as major time series of national figures from 1949-1988.

76. Sullivan, Lawrence R. *Historical dictionary of the People's Republic of China, 1949-1997.* Lanham, MD : Scarecrow Press, 1997. 279 p.

77. Tang, Raymond N. and Wei-yi Ma, comps. *Source materials on Red Guard and the Great Proletarian Cultural Revolution.* Ann Arbor : The University of Michigan, 1969. 332 leaves.
     Part I is a bibliography of Red Guard publications which had become available up to 1969. Part II is a listing of the titles of the chief articles in these publications.

78. Townsend, James R. and Richard Bush, comps. *People's Republic of China : a basic handbook.* 2nd ed. New York : Council on International and Public Affairs, in cooperation with the China Council of the Asia Society, 1981. 112 p.

79. Wang, James C. F. *The cultural revolution in China : an annotated bibliography.* New York : Garland Publishing Inc., 1976. 246 p.
     Covers the Cultural Revolution in the period of 1966-1969. Lists books, monographs, and journal articles in English, and includes a wide range of topics related to the revolution and its impact on China.

80. *Who's who in Communist China.* Revised ed. Hong Kong : Union Research Institute, 1969-1970. 2 v. (897 p.).
     Contains a total of 2,837 biographies and includes appendixes listing the membership of the 9th Chinese Communist Party Central Committee, provincial revolutionary committees, the military leaders and the central government organizations between 1949 and 1969.

II

General Works

81. An, Pyong-jun. *Chinese politics and the Cultural Revolution : dynamics of policy process.* Seattle : University of Washington Press, 1976. 392 p.
Traces the origins of the Cultural Revolution dealing with the eight-year period between 1958 to 1966, and also outlines the process of making and implementing the revolution between 1965 and 1966.

82. Barnouin, Barbara and Yu Changgen. *Ten years of turbulence : the Chinese cultural revolution.* London ; New York : K. Paul International ; New York : Distributed by Routledge, Chapman & Hall Inc., 1993. 369 p.
An analysis of the process of the Cultural Revolution. Examines major events in the ten years of turbulence, from the "5.16 Circular" and the fall of Liu Shaoqi to the Lin Biao Affair and the elimination of the Gang of Four. Emphasizes the role of Mao Zedong in launching and leading the Cultural Revolution.

83. Bennett, Gordon A. *Yundong : mass campaigns in Chinese communist leadership.* Berkeley : Center for Chinese Studies, University of California, 1976. 133 p.
This study reaches three broad conclusions about the role and importance of mass campaigns: provide citizens with an effective vehicle for political participation; contribute more to economic growth than take away; continue to thrive in Chinese politics following the leadership succession to Mao Zedong and his generation of revolutionary cadres.

84. Blecher, Marc J. *China : politics, economics and society : iconoclasm and innovation in a revolutionary socialist country.* Boulder, CO : Rienner, 1986. 232 p.

An interpretation of development in China since 1949. There is a detailed description of the Socialist Education Movement of the early 1960's, Mao Zedong's perspective of the Two-line struggle, and the Cultural Revolution.

85.   Blecher, Marc J. and Gordon White. *Micropolitics in contemporary China : technical unit during and after the Cultural Revolution.* White Plains, NY : M.E. Sharpe, 1979. 135 p.
Based upon interviews in Hong Kong with a Chinese worker. Describes the situation in a technical unit during and after the Cultural Revolution. Analyzes the political dynamics of the movement and political changes. Focuses on the character of basic level political process and the relationship to national political movement.

86.   Brown, Cheryl Luvenia. *Restoring a one-party regime in China : a study of party branches, 1964-1978.* Thesis (Ph.D.). University of Michigan, 1983. 487 leaves.

87.   Brugger, Bill. *China : radicalism to revisionism, 1962-1979.* London : Croom Helm, 1981. 275 p.
Traces the split in the leadership of Chinese Communist Party after 1962 and documents the breakdown of the Chinese leadership consensus.

88.   Butterfield, Fox. *China, alive in the bitter sea.* New York : Times Books, c1982. 468 p.
The author stationed in Beijing as a New York Times reporter. This work covers all aspects of Chinese life in the Cultural Revolution and the aftermath. Information came from Chinese documents, from books on China by Western authorities, from author's observations, and from accounts by his many Chinese contacts.

89.   Butterfield, Fox. *China, alive in the bitter sea.* Revised and updated ed. New York : Times Books, 1990. 492 p.

90.   Cell, Charles P. *Revolution at work : mobilization campaigns in China.* New York : Academic Press, 1977. 221 p.
Studies the campaign, its component process of mobilization, and its outcomes, both shortcomings and achievements.

91.   Chang, Yi-Chun. *Factional and coalition politics in China : Cultural Revolution and its aftermath.* New York : Praeger, 1976. 144 p.

Examines the major factions and coalitions that had vied for control of the party and government during the Cultural Revolution.

92.   *Chinese Cultural Revolution*. [Hong Kong? : s.n.], 1996. 1 v.
Photocopies of 10 papers presented at a conference held at the Hong Kong University of Science and Technology, July 4-6, 1996.

93.   Chu, Godwin C., Philip H. Cheng, and Leonard Chu. *The roles of tatzepao in the Cultural Revolution : a structural-functional analysis.* Carbondale : Southern Illinois University, 1972. 45, 6 p.
Analyzes the roles of tatzepao (Dazibao; big-character wall posters) in the Cultural Revolution mass movement.

94.   Collier, John. *Dynamics of socialism*. London : Marram Books ; Atlantic Highlands, NJ : Distributed in the U.S. and Canada by Humanities Press, 1986. 202 p.
Discusses the socialism in general, and attempts to explain and defend the particular Chinese experience.

95.   D'Avray, Anthony. *Red China through Mao's long march to the cultural revolution : a phased historical case study in problem solving and decision making*. London : AEM Publishers, 1978. 104 p.

96.   Dittmer, Lowell. *China's continuous revolution : the post-liberation epoch, 1949-1981*. Berkeley ; Los Angeles : University of California Press, 1987. 320 p.
Examines the persistence of revolutionary politics in China after 1949. Analyzes the political and social transformation during the 1949-1965 period, emphasizes the political movement during the 1966-1968 period, and gives particular attention to the late Cultural Revolution period after 1968.

97.   Dittmer, Lowell and Chen Ruoxi. *Ethics and rhetoric of the Chinese Cultural Revolution*. Berkeley, CA : Center for Chinese Studies, Institute of East Asian Studies, University of California, 1981. 127 p.
An essay on the cultural impact of the Cultural Revolution to include the entire 1966 to 1976 decade.

98.   Edwards, R. Randle, Louis Henkin, and Andrew J. Nathan. *Human rights in contemporary China*. New York : Columbia University Press, 1986. 193 p.

99.   Fan, Kuang Huan and K. T. Fan, eds. *From the other side of the river : a portrait of China today.* New York : Doubleday, 1975. 429 p.
       Covers various topics including family and marriage, population policy, women's liberation, maternity and child care, the school child, people's communes, cities, industrial and agriculture movement, commerce and finance, revolution in education, movement to criticize Lin Biao and Confucius, and others.

100.   Feng Jicai. *Ten years of madness : oral histories of China's Cultural Revolution.* 1st ed. San Francisco : China Books & Periodicals, 1996. 285 p.
       Translation of: Yi bai ge ren di shi nian (selections).
       Includes the testimonies of fifteen people from all walks of life, from Red Guards and rebels to workers and intellectuals, who were persecuted during the Cultural Revolution. It also includes appendixes: Cultural Revolution in the eyes of the new generation; an interview with the author Feng Jicai; a chronology of events (1949-1979); key figures of the Cultural Revolution.

101.   Feng Jicai. *Voices from the whirlwind : an oral history of the Chinese Cultural Revolution.* 1st ed. New York : Pantheon Books ; Beijing : Foreign Languages Press, c1991. 252 p.
       Translation of: Yi bai ge ren di shi nian (selections).

102.   Fox, Galen. *Campaigning for power in China during the Cultural Revolution era, 1967-1976.* Thesis (Ph.D.). Princeton University, 1978. 392 leaves.

103.   Fu Zhengyuan. *Autocratic tradition and Chinese politics.* Cambridge, England ; New York : Cambridge University Press, 1993. 401 p.
       Contents include: The Great Proletarian Cultural Revolution, 1966-1976; Prelude to the Cultural Revolution; The rise and fall of the Red Guards; New alignment and conflict; The April 5 Tianamen Square incident; Some thoughts on the Cultural Revolution.

104.   Gong Xiaoxia. *Repressive movements and the politics of victimization : patronage and persecution during the cultural revolution.* Thesis (Ph.D.). Harvard University, 1995. 312 leaves.

105.   Goodstadt, Leo. *China's Watergate : political and economic conflict, 1969-1977.* New Delhi : Vikas ; Atlantic Highlands, NJ : Distributed in the U.S. by Humanities Press, 1979. 219 p.

106. Gordner, John. *Chinese politics and succession to Mao.* New York : Holmes and Meier Publishers, 1984. 217 p.
Examines the major events since the 1950s that led to the changes in China's leadership. Relates the chaos of the Cultural Revolution to the struggles of specific personalities for control of mass movements and for the favor of Mao Zedong.

107. Gudoshnikov, L. M. (Leonid Moiseevich), R. M. Neronov, and B. P. Barakhta. *China : cultural revolution and after.* New Delhi : Sterling, c1978. 248 p.

108. Guillermaz, Jacques. *Chinese Communist Party in power, 1949-1976.* Boulder, CO : Westview Press, 1976. 614 p.
Translation of: Le parti communiste chinois au pouvoir.
Contents include "The Socialist Education Movement and the Cultural Revolution and its aftermath, 1962-1976."

109. Harding, Harry. *Organizing China : the problem of bureaucracy 1949-1976.* Stanford, CA : Stanford University Press, 1981. 418 p.
Examines the problems China encountered in building and maintaining effective administrative organizations. Contains a series of studies of policy issues including agriculture, public health, education, cultural and intellectual affairs, military policy, and industrial management.

110. Ho, Ping-ti and Tang Tsou, eds. *China in crisis.* Chicago : University of Chicago Press, 1968. 2 v.
Contents: v. 1. *China's heritage and the communist political system.* v. 2. *China's policies in Asia and America's alternatives.*
The first volume focuses on the conditions that led to the Communist victory in 1949, and examines the Communist political system. The second volume includes analyses of the Chinese political system, the Cultural Revolution, economic development, and foreign policy.

111. Hunter, Iris. *They made revolution within the revolution : the story of Great Proletarian Cultural Revolution.* Chicago : RCP Publications, 1986. 61 p.

112. Joseph, William A. *The critique of ultra-leftism in China, 1958-1981.* Stanford, CA : Stanford University Press, 1984. 328 p.
A study of the anti-leftist criticism in modern Chinese history including the Great Leap Forward Campaign of 1958-1960, and the Cultural Revolution of 1966-1976.

113. Joseph, William A., Christine P. W. Wong, and David Zweig, eds. *New perspectives on the Cultural Revolution*. Cambridge, MA : Council on East Asian Studies, Harvard University : Distributed by Harvard University Press, 1991. 351 p.
      Contents include: Cultural Revolution radicalism; Agrarian radicalism as a rural development strategy; Factional politics in Zhejiang, 1973-1976; Neither plan nor market: Mao's political economy; Industrial policy during the Cultural Revolution; Central-provincial investment and finance: the Cultural Revolution and its legacy in Jiangsu Province; Arts policies of the Cultural Revolution; Dramas of passion: heroism in the Cultural Revolution's model, etc.

114. Leys, Simon. *Broken images : essays on Chinese culture and politics.* New York : St. Martin's Press, 1980. 156 p.
      A collection of essays and vignettes originally published between 1974 and 1977 on the aspects of Chinese culture and politics.

115. Leys, Simon. *The Chairman's new clothes : Mao and the cultural revolution.* London : Allison and Busby, 1977. 261 p.
      Translation of: Les habits neufs du President Mao.
      Part one of the book gives a historical perspective describing and analyzing the origins of the Cultural Revolution. Part two contains "A Diary of the Cultural Revolution through 1967, 1968 and 1969." Appendixes include several documents related to the Cultural Revolution.

116. Leys, Simon. *The Chairman's new clothes : Mao and the cultural revolution.* Rev. ed. London ; New York : Allison & Busby ; Schocken Books [distributor], 1981. 272 p.

117. Lin Weiran. *An abortive Chinese enlightenment : the Cultural Revolution and class theory.* Thesis (Ph.D.). University of Wisconsin-Madison, 1996. 462 leaves.

118. Lipman, Jonathan N. and Stevan Harrell, eds. *Violence in China : essays in culture and counterculture.* Albany : State University of New York Press, 1990. 249 p.
      Based on papers presented at a panel held at the Annual Meeting of the Association for Asian Studies in Philadelphia in 1985. Contents include: Urban violence during the Cultural Revolution : who is to blame / Anne F. Thurston. The politics of revenge in rural China during the Cultural Revolution / Richard Madsen.

119. Liu Guokai; Anita Chan, ed. *A brief analysis of the Cultural Revolution.* Armonk, NY : M.E. Sharpe, c1987. 151 p.
An abridged translated version of the author's essay originally published in the special issue no. 2 (Dec. 1980) of Ren min zhi sheng (People's Voice). Three major themes were discussed in the book: why there were two diametrically opposed factions; moral evaluation; and sorting out the complex relationship between the political elite and the populace during the chaos.

120. Liu, Judith. *Life out of balance : the Chinese cultural revolution and modernization.* Thesis (Ph.D.). University of California, San Diego, 1985. 257 leaves.

121. MacFarquhar, Roderick. *The origins of the cultural revolution.* New York : Published for the Royal Institute of International Affairs, the East Asian Institute of Columbia University, and the Research Institute on Communist Affairs of Columbia University by Columbia University Press, 1974-1997. 3 v.
Contents: v. 1. Contradictions among the people, 1956-1957. v. 2. The great leap forward, 1958-1960. v. 3. The coming of the cataclysm, 1961-1966.

122. MacFarquhar, Roderick. *The origins of the cultural revolution in China: the dispute over 'Liberalisation', 1956-1957.* Thesis (Ph.D.). London School of Economics and Political Science, 1980. 247 p.

123. MacFarquhar, Roderick and John K. Fairbank, eds. *People's Republic, Part 2 : revolutions within the Chinese revolution, 1966-1982.* Cambridge ; New York : Cambridge University Press, 1991. 1,108 p.
This volume is v. 15, pt. 2 of *The Cambridge History of China.*
Contents include: Mao Tse-tung's thought from 1949-1976; The succession of Mao and the end of Maoism; The opening to America; China's economic policy and performance; Education; Creativity and politics; Urban life in the People's Republic; Literature under communism; Taiwan under Nationalist rule, 1949-1982.

124. Maitan, Livio. *Party, army, and masses in China : Marxist interpretation of the cultural revolution and its aftermath.* London : NLB ; Atlantic Highlands, NJ : Humanities Press, 1976. 373 p.
Translation of: Partito, esercito e masse nella crisi cinese.

Contents include: The context 1949-1965; the three years of the Cultural Revolution; aftermath of the Cultural Revolution; and an appendix (Interview with a Cantonese Red Guard / by Tariq Ali).

125. Marchant, Leslie Ronald. *The turbulent giant : communist theory and practice in China*. Sydney : Australia and New Zealand Book Co., 1975. 131 p.

126. Meisner, Maurice J. *Mao's China and after : a history of the People's Republic*. New York : Free Press ; London : Collier Macmillan, 1986. 534 p.
      A revised and expanded edition of: Mao's China, 1977.
      Presents a detailed account of the Cultural Revolution. Examines the social consequence of the violent upheaval in the Cultural Revolution and traces those political events from the fall of Lin Biao to the fall of the Gang of Four. Also examines the post-Mao era up to 1984.

127. Moody, Peter R. *Opposition and dissent in contemporary China*. Stanford, CA : Hoover Institution Press, 1977. 342 p.

128. *New China's first quarter-century*. Peking : Foreign Languages Press, 1975. 209 p.
      Contents include topics of Shanghai's industry, Daqing oil zone and Dazhai, revolution in education, development in science and technology, barefoot doctor system, and others.

129. *New perspectives on the Cultural Revolution : May 15-17, 1987*. Cambridge, MA : Harvard University, John King Fairbank Center for East Asian Research, 1987. 2 v.

130. Pietrusza, David. *Chinese Cultural Revolution*. San Diego, CA : Lucent Books, 1996. 96 p.

131. *Resolution on CPC history (1949-1981)*. 1st ed. Beijing : Foreign Languages Press, 1981. 126 p.
      On cover: Authoritative assessment of Mao Zedong, the cultural revolution, achievement of the People's Republic.
      Contents include: 1. Resolution on certain questions in the history of our party since the founding of the People's Republic China. 2. Speech at the meeting in celebration of the anniversary of the sixtieth anniversary of the founding of the Chinese Communist Party—by Hu Yaobang. 3.

Communiqué of the sixth plenary session of the 11th Central Committee of the CCP.

132. *Resolution on CPC history (1949-1981)*. 1st ed. Oxford ; New York : Pergamon Press, 1981. 126 p.

133. *Rethinking the "Cultural Revolution."* Beijing, China : Beijing Review, 1987. 71 p.

134. *Revolution is dead, long live the revolution : readings on the great proletarian cultural revolution from an ultra-left perspective.* Hong Kong : The 70's, 1976. 291 p.
Contents include: The great proletarian cultural revolution and the reversal of workers' power in China; Mao's China and the proletarian cultural revolution; The explosion point of ideology in China; Sheng-Wu-Lien, Whither China; An interview with an ultra-leftist; Concerning socialist democracy and legal system; Some thoughts on the Chinese revolution.

135. Salisbury, Harrison Evans. *The new emperors : China in the era of Mao and Deng.* Boston : Little, Brown, 1992. 544 p.
Provides a detailed picture of the personal relationships and private lives of China's highest officers of the past 40 years.

136. Schoenhals, Michael, ed. *Mao's great inquisition : the central case examination group, 1966-1979.* Armonk, NY : Sharpe, 1996. 95 p.
It was published as Chinese Law and Government, vol. 29, no. 3 (May/June, 1996).

137. Seybolt, Peter J., ed. *Through Chinese eyes.* New York : Praeger, 1974. 2 v. (294 p.)
Contents: v. 1. Revolution: a nation stand up. v. 2. Transformation: building a new society.
Contains selections from Chinese fiction, poetry, autobiography and political commentary covering various subjects related to the Cultural Revolution.

138. Sharma, K. R. *China : revolution to revolution.* 1st ed. New Delhi, India : Mittal Publications, 1989. 266 p.

139.   Solomon, Richard H., with Talbott W. Huey. *A revolution is not a dinner party : a feast of images of the Maoist transformation of China.* 1st ed. Garden City, NY : Anchor Press, 1975. 199 p.

140.   Teiwes, Frederick C. *Leadership, legitimacy, and conflict in China : from a charismatic Mao to the politics of succession.* Armonk, NY : M.E. Sharpe, 1984. 169 p.
       Three essays address the leadership politics at the Chinese political system.

141.   Topper, Henry. *From the commune to the cultural revolution : a discussion of party leadership and democracy in Lenin and Mao.* Thesis (Ph.D.). Johns Hopkins University, 1991. 339 leaves.

142.   Tsou, Tang. *The Cultural Revolution and post-Mao reforms : a historical perspective.* Chicago : University of Chicago Press, 1986. 351 p.

143.   Walder, Andrew George and Gong Xiaoxia, eds. *China's great terror : new documentation on the Cultural Revolution.* Armonk, NY : M.E. Sharpe, 1993. 103 p.
       Articles collected and translated in this volume all appeared in official Chinese sources between 1979-1991, and document these systematic persecutions in vivid detail. This volume was published as Chinese sociology and anthropology, vol. 26, no. 1 (Fall 1993).

144.   Waller, Derek J. *The government and politics of communist China.* New York : New York University Press, 1981. 228 p.

145.   Wedeman, Andrew Hall. *The east wind subsides : Chinese foreign policy and the origins of the Cultural Revolution.* Washington, DC : Washington Institute Press, c1987. 317 p.
       Describes the struggles in Chinese politics during the 1960s, and examines those complex events leading up to the Cultural Revolution.

146.   White, Lynn T. *Policies of chaos : the organizational causes of violence in China's cultural revolution.* Princeton, NJ : Princeton University Press, c1989. 367 p.
       Centers on groups of 'workers' and 'managers,' 'students' and 'residents,' and overviews the period of 1949 to 1966 and 1966 to 1968 covering many angles in seeking the causes of the Cultural Revolution.

147. White, Lynn T. *Politics of class and class origin : the case of the Cultural Revolution*. Canberra, Australia : Australian National University, 1976. 97 p.

148. Wong-Sandor, Helen Ka-shing. *Paths to political leadership in the People's Republic of China, 1966-1976 : thirteen cases*. Thesis (Ph.D.). University of Melbourne, 1984. 580 p.

149. Yan Jiaqi and Gao Gao. *The ten-year history of the Chinese cultural revolution*. 1st ed. Taipei : Institute of Current China Studies, 1988. 617 p.
      Translation of: Zhong guo "wen ge" shi nian shi.
      A comprehensive narrative account of the Cultural Revolution.

150. Yan Jiaqi and Gao Gao. *Turbulent decade : a history of the cultural revolution*. Honolulu : University of Hawaii Press, c1996. 659 p.
      Translation of: Zhong guo "wen ge" shi nian shi.
      Based on the revised edition, and was edited and translated by D.W.Y. Kwok in consultation with the authors. Contains an introduction by Kwok.

151. Zhelokhovtsev, Aleksei Nikolaevich. *The "cultural revolution" : a close-up : an eyewitness account*. Moscow : Progress Publishers, 1975. 244 p.
      Translation of: Kul'turnaia revoliutslia s blizkogo rasstoianiia.

III

Special Periods

A. GREAT CHAOS, 1966-1969

152. *Absorb proletarian fresh blood : an important question in party consolidation.* Peking : Foreign Languages Press, 1968. 26 p.
Translation of: Xi shou wu chan jie ji de xin xian xue ye, which was originally issued as an editorial of Hongqi on October 14, 1968.

153. Adhikari, G. *What do they want to achieve by this 'cultural revolution.'* New Delhi : D.P. Sinha for Communist Party of India, 1966. 39 p.

154. *Advance along the road opened up by the October Socialist revolution : in commemoration of the 50th anniversary of the great October Socialist Revolution.* Peking : Foreign Languages Press, 1967. 27 p.
Contents include Lin Biao's speech at the Beijing rally commemorating the 50th anniversary of the October Revolution on Nov. 6, 1967, and an editorial of Renmin Ribao, Hongqi, and Jiefangjun Bao (Nov. 6, 1967).

155. *Advance courageously along the road of victory : in warm celebration of the 19th anniversary of the founding of the People's Republic of China.* Peking : Foreign Languages Press, 1968. 30 p.

156. *Along the socialist or the capitalist road?* Peking : Foreign Languages Press, 1968. 45 p.

157. An, Tai Sung. *Mao Tse-tung's Cultural Revolution.* Indianapolis : Pegasus, 1972. 211 p.
Describes and analyzes the progress of the Cultural Revolution up to 1970. Appendixes list members of the Ninth Central Committee of the

Chinese Communist Party, and leading members of the revolutionary committee in the major provinces and cities.

158. *An epoch-making document : in commemoration of the second anniversary of the publication of the circular.* Peking : Foreign Languages Press, 1968. 14 p.
It was originally issued as an editorial of Renmin Ribao, Hongqi, and Jiefangjun Bao, in commemoration of the second anniversary of the publication of the Circular of the Central Committee of the Chinese communist Party (May 16, 1966).

159. Asia Research Centre, comp. & ed.. *Great cultural revolution in China.* Rutland, VT : C. E. Tuttle Co., 1968. 507 p.
Contains a series of Chinese official documents dealing with the origins and development of the Cultural Revolution from 1963 to 1966. Includes a directory of key Chinese officials involved in the early stages of the Cultural Revolution, a glossary of the special political terms, slogans used in the Cultural Revolution, and a chronology of the major events from November 1965 to November 1966.
Sequel: Great power struggle in China.

160. Barcata, Louis. *China in the throes of the cultural revolution : an eye witness report.* New York : Hart Publishing Co., 1968. 299 p.
Translation of: China in der Kulturrevolution.
Based largely on a visit made in the Spring of 1967.

161. Baum, Richard and Louise B. Bennett, eds. *China in ferment : perspectives on the cultural revolution.* Englewood Cliffs, NJ : Prentice-Hall, 1971. 246 p.
A collection of articles on the origins, development and trends of the Cultural Revolution in the period of 1966-1969. Includes Lin Biao's report to the Chinese Communist Party's Ninth National Congress in April 1969.

162. *Behind China's Great Cultural Revolution.* New York : Merit Publishers, 1967. 63 p.
Contains four articles published between August 1966 and February 1967: Peng Shu-tse on background of Chinese events; Second interview with Peng Shu-tse: Mao's Cultural Revolution; Meaning of Shanghai events; The upheaval in China, an analysis of the contending force.

163.   Bennett, Gordon. *China's continuing revolution : will it be permanent?*
Berkeley : Center for Chinese Studies, University of California, 1970. 17
p.
In review the events in China for the year of 1969.

164.   Britton, Dale Gregory. *Chairman Mao and the Red Guard : a "top and
bottom" alliance against the CCP bureaucracy, June to December
1966.* Thesis (M.A.). University of Virginia, 1992. 144 leaves.

165.   *Carry the great proletarian cultural revolution through to the end.*
Peking : Foreign Languages Press, 1967. 57 p.
Translation of: Ba wu chan jie ji wen hua da ge ming jin xing dao di,
which was issued as a New Year's editorial for 1967 by Renmin Ribao
and Hongqi.

166.   Chang Hsin-cheng. *Evening chats at Yenshan; or, the case of Teng To.*
Berkeley : Center for Chinese Studies, University of California, 1970. 56
p.

167.   Chang Hsin-cheng. *The Great Proletarian Cultural Revolution : a
terminological study.* Berkeley : University of California Press, 1967. 72
p.

168.   Chang, Parris H. *Radicals and radical ideology in China's cultural
revolution.* New York : Research Institute on Communist Affairs, School
of International Affairs, Columbia University, 1973. 103 p.
Gives a comprehensive account of the factional infighting along
ideological lines in the Cultural Revolution, and profiles of some
Chinese radical leaders from Jiang Qing and Chen Boda down to Wang
Li and Guan Feng.

169.   Chang, Teh-kuang. *Cultural revolution and the political modernization
of Communist China : prepared for delivery at the 8th World Congress
of the International Political Association, Munich, Federal German
Republic, August 31-September 5, 1970.* [S.l.] : International Political
Science Association, 1970. 42 leaves.

170.   Chen, Jack. *Inside the Cultural Revolution.* New York : Macmillan,
1975. 483 p.
The author worked in China from 1950-1970 as a journalist, editor, and
artist. This work covers the phases of the Cultural Revolution from its
earliest manifestations to the Lin Biao affair (1966-1971).

171. Chen Yung-sheng. *Brutalities committed by the Red Guards = Hung wei ping pao hsing chen hsiang*. Taipei : Chung-kuo ching nien fan kung chiu kuo tuan tsung tuan pu, [1969?]. 1 v.
Pictorial works.

172. Chi, Wen-shun, comp. *Readings in the Chinese Communist Cultural Revolution : a manual for students of the Chinese language*. Berkeley : University of California Press, 1971. 530 p.
Contains 21 documents which were selected from Chinese publications published during the period of 1965-1968. The first category is official documents dealing with the Cultural Revolution. The second is journal articles about ideological conflicts among Chinese leaders.

173. *China after the cultural revolution : a selection from the Bulletin of the Atomic Scientists*. New York : Random House, 1969. 247 p.

174. Chiu, Chui-liang. *Maoism in action : the Cultural Revolution*. St. Lucia : University of Queensland Press ; New York : Crane, Russak, 1974. 176 p.
It was originally presented as the author's thesis (Ph.D. California-Riverside, 1971) under the title: *Ideology and political power in Mao Tse-tung's Cultural Revolution, 1965-1968*.

175. *Commemorating Lu Hsun : our forerunner in the Cultural Revolution*. Peking : Foreign Languages Press, 1967. 48 p.

176. *Cultural revolution in China : its origins and course*. New York : C. Scribner, 1967. 61 p.
At head of title: Keesing's research report.

177. Daubier, Jean. *A history of the Chinese Cultural Revolution*. New York : Vintage Books, 1974. 336 p.
Translation of: Histoire de la revolution culturelle proletarienne en Chine, 1965-1969. Translated from French by Richard Seaver.
A detailed account of the development during the Cultural Revolution based upon Chinese sources and author's own firsthand knowledge of these events as a participant. The author was a French translator for the Chinese government during the period of 1966 and 1968.

178. Deliusin, Lev Petrovich. *The "cultural revolution" in China*. Moscow : Novosti Press Agency Publishing House, 1967. 103 p.
Translation of: "Kul'turnaia revoliutsiia" v Kitae.

179. *Diary of the Great Cultural Revolution, Oct. '66-Apr. '67.* Tokyo : Asahi Evening News, 1967. 95 p.
Other title: *Diary of the cultural revolution, Oct. '66-Apr. '67.*

180. Dorrill, William F. *Power, policy, and ideology in the making of China's "cultural revolution."* Santa Monica, CA : Rand Corp., 1968. 151 p.

181. Doyle, Jean Louise. *Conflict management in the Chinese Cultural Revolution : a case study in political change.* Thesis (Ph.D.). Boston University, 1973. 315 leaves.

182. Dutt, Gargi and Vidya Prakash Dutt. *China's cultural revolution.* New York : Asia Publishing House, 1970. 260 p.
Traces the origins and development of the Cultural Revolution from the Great Leap Forward (1958-1960) to 1969. Gives a full picture of the upheaval for the period of 1966-1969.

183. Elegant, Robert S. *Mao's great revolution.* New York ; Cleveland : World Publishing Company, 1971. 478 p.
Provides a comprehensive narrative account of the Cultural Revolution beginning with the Lushan Conference in 1959. Describes in detail how the attacks of Peng Zhen and Wang Guangmei (wife of Liu Shaoqi) were started, and how the criticism campaign in Beijing's universities was launched, and how the student movement expanded into a violent rebellion and a power seizure. Many of the materials used for this book are Chinese official documents and Red Guard publications. Includes excerpts from the three "trials" of Wang Guangmei during the day and night of April 10, 1967 (p.347-367).

184. Esmein, Jean. *The Chinese cultural revolution.* 1st ed. Garden City, NY : Anchor Press, 1973. 346 p.
Translation of : La revolution culturelle chinoise.
A detailed account of the development of the Cultural Revolution based upon a variety of documented sources. The author was the press attaché of the French Embassy in Beijing in the early period of the Cultural Revolution.

185. *Fight for the further consolidation of the dictatorship of the proletariat : in celebration of the 20th anniversary of the founding of the People's Republic of China.* Peking : Foreign Languages Press, 1969. 41 p.

186. Fokkema, Douwe Wessel. *Report from Peking : observations of a Western diplomat on the cultural revolution.* Montreal : McGill-Queen's University Press, 1972. 185 p.
Translation of: Standplaats in Peking.
The author lived in Beijing as the Charge d'Affaire for the Office of Netherlands Charge d'Affaires. His narrative runs up to the Ninth Chinese Communist Party Congress in April, 1969.

187. *Follow Chairman Mao and advance in the teeth of great storms and waves.* Peking : Foreign Languages Press, 1967. 14 p.

188. *Forward along the high road of Mao Tse-tung's thought : in celebration of the 17th anniversary of the founding of the People's Republic of China.* Peking : Foreign Languages Press, 1967. 36 p.

189. Granqvist, Hans. *The Red Guard : a report on Mao's revolution.* New York : F. A. Praeger, 1967. 159 p.
Translation and updating of: Kinas Roda garde.

190. Gray, Jack and Patrick Cavendish. *Chinese communism in crisis : Maoism and the cultural revolution.* New York : Praeger, 1968. 279 p.
Studies the major events and issues of the 1966-1967 crisis in China. Some sources used in this work are from Red Guard posters, pamphlets and newspapers. The appendix, approximately half the book, contains twelve documentary sources including Wu Han's *the Dismissal of Hai Jui,* Yao Wenyuan's *On the new historical drama--the Dismissal of Hai Jui,* and other articles.

191. *Great power struggle in China.* Hong Kong : Asia Research Centre, 1969. 503 p.
A collection of official documents, radio broadcasts, and speeches by Chinese Communist Party leaders between 1967 and 1968, arranged under nine headings: The Red Guard movement; Spread of the revolution to the countryside and to industrial and mining enterprises; January Revolution; Nationwide struggle to seize power; Reverse in the power struggle; the Impact of the power struggle; the Army's role in Cultural Revolution; the Cultural Revolution in the army; the Problem involving the army.
A sequel to the book "The great cultural revolution in China."

192. *Great proletarian cultural revolution in China.* Peking, China : Foreign Languages Press; 1967-1969. 3 v.

Continues: Great socialist cultural revolution in China.

193. *Great socialist cultural revolution in China.* Peking : Foreign Languages
      Press. 1966-1967. 7 v.

194. *Great strategic concept.* Peking : Foreign Languages Press, 1967. 50 p.

195. *Great victory for Chairman Mao's revolutionary line : warmly hail the
      birth of Peking Municipal Revolutionary Committee.* Peking : Foreign
      Languages Press, 1967. 88 p.
      A collection of speeches by Zhou Enlai, Jiang Qing, Xie Fuzhi and
      others, together with editorials from Renmin Ribao, Jiefangjun Bao,
      Hongqi on the establishment of the Beijing Municipal Revolutionary
      Committee, April 20, 1967.

196. Gunawardhana, Theja. *China's Cultural Revolution.* Colombo : s.n.,
      1967. 264 p.

197. Harding, Harry. *Maoist theories of policy-making and organization :
      lessons from the Cultural Revolution.* Santa Monica, CA : Rand, 1969.
      39 p.
      A report prepared for the United States Air Force project.

198. Harding, Harry. *Modernization and Mao : the logic of the Cultural
      Revolution and the 1970s.* Santa Monica, CA : Rand, 1970. 21 leaves.

199. Heaslet, Juliana Pennington. *The Cultural Revolution, 1966-1969 : the
      failure of Mao's Revolution in China.* Thesis (Ph.D.). University of
      Colorado, 1971. 221 leaves.

200. Hinton, Harold C. *Policymaking and the power struggle in Communist
      China during the Cultural Revolution.* Arlington, VA : Institute for
      Defense Analyzes, International and Social Studies Division, 1968. 43
      leaves.

201. Hinton, William. *Turning point in China : an essay on the cultural
      revolution.* New York : Monthly Review Press, 1972. 112 p.
      Tries to explain that the Cultural Revolution was launched by Mao
      Zedong to resolve the contradictions of the Chinese people and the
      bourgeoisie.

202.   *Hold aloft the banner of unity of the party's ninth congress and win still greater victories.* Peking : Foreign Languages Press, 1969. 17 p.

203.   Hsia, Adrian. *The Chinese cultural revolution.* 1st American ed. New York : McGraw-Hill, 1972. 254 p.
Examines the major events in the Cultural Revolution, and focuses mainly on the contradictions and stresses in various strata of Chinese society during the Cultural Revolution.
Translation of : Die chinesische Kulturrevolution.

204.   Hsiao, Gene T. *The background and development of the proletarian cultural revolution.* Berkeley : Center for Chinese Studies, Institute of International Studies, University of California, 1967. 389-404 p.
Reprinted from Asian Survey, vol. 7, no. 6 (June 1967).

205.   Hsiung, Yin Tso. *Red China's cultural revolution.* 1st ed. New York : Vantage Press, 1968. 188 p.
Focuses on the complexities of Mao Zedong's thought, and examines the role of the individuals and factions in China.

206.   Huang Shaorong. *To rebel is justified : a rhetorical study of China's cultural revolution movement, 1966-1969.* Lanham, MD : University Press of America, 1996. 221 p.

207.   Huberman, Leo and Paul Seezy. *The cultural revolution in China : a socialist analysis.* Ann Arbor, MI : Radical Education Project, [1966?]. 17 p.

208.   Hunter, Neale. *Shanghai journal : an eyewitness account of the Cultural Revolution.* New York : Praeger, 1969. 311 p.
A personal eyewitness account of the Cultural Revolution in Shanghai, where the author taught English at the Shanghai Foreign Languages Institute from November 1965 to April 1967.
"Key to Red Guard newspapers cited in the text": p. 302-307.

209.   Hunter, Neale. *Shanghai journal : an eyewitness account of the Cultural Revolution.* Hong Kong ; New York : Oxford University Press, 1988. 311 p.
With a new introduction by the author.

210. Hwang, Tien-chien. *1967, a year of precariousness for Chinese Communists*. Taipei : Asian Peoples' Anti-Communist League, 1968. 98 p.

211. Hwang, Tien-chien. *Analysis of the "Cultural Revolution" of CCP in 1966*. Taipei : Asian Peoples' Anti-Communist League, 1966. 2 v.

212. Hwang, Tien-chien. *Transformation of Mao-Lin faction's tactical line for power seizure*. Taipei : Asian Peoples' Anti-Communist League, 1968. 94 p.

213. Johnson, Chalmers A. *China : the cultural revolution in structural perspectives*. Berkeley : Center for Chinese Studies, 1968. 15 p.
      Reprinted from Asian Survey, vol. 8, no. 1 (January 1968).

214. Karol, K. S. *The second Chinese revolution*. London : Jonathan Cape, 1975. 472 p.
      The author visited China in 1965 and 1971. It is a critical account of the Chinese Cultural Revolution through to the fall of Lin Biao in 1971.

215. Kato, Hiroki. *The Red Guard movement, May, 1966-January, 1967 : a case of a student movement in China*. Thesis (Ph.D.). University of Chicago, 1974. 150 leaves.

216. Lee, Hong Yung. *The political mobilization of the Red Guards and revolutionary rebels in the Cultural Revolution*. Thesis (Ph.D.). University of Chicago, 1973. 657 leaves.

217. Lee, Hong Yung. *The politics of the Chinese cultural revolution : a case study*. Berkeley : University of California Press, 1978. 369 p.
      An account of the Red Guard and worker-rebel factions, the battles, and power seizures that took place in China from 1966 to 1968.

218. Lee, Hong Yung. *Structures of conflict in the Red Guard movement : utility and limitation of the Red Guard newspapers as source materials*. Berkeley, CA : s.n., 1974. 55 leaves.

219. Lewis, John Wilson, ed. *Party leadership and revolutionary power in China*. Cambridge, England : University Press, 1970. 422 p.
      Contains twelve essays written by British and American scholars for a 1968 conference on the Chinese Communist Party. Discusses China's political system, factionalism within the Central Committee, leadership

problems, policies toward intellectuals, and army-party relations in light of the Cultural Revolution.

220. Liao Kuang-sheng. *Internal mobilization and external hostility in Communist China, 1949-1962 and 1967-1969.* Thesis (Ph.D.). University of Michigan, 1974. 307 leaves.

221. Lin Jing. *The Red Guards' path to violence : political, educational, and psychological factors.* New York : Praeger, 1991. 187 p.
Studies the political, educational, and psychological factors inherent in the Red Guards' thinking, particularly about class struggle in the Cultural Revolution, and considers new alternative modes of thinking necessary, if features of that tragic event are not to be repeated.

222. Lindbeck, John M. H., ed. *China : management of a revolutionary society.* Seattle : University of Washington Press. 1971. 391 p.
Consists of a collection of nine studies on the relationship between leaders and masses, central authority and provincial level, economic management, the role of the military, the management of foreign affairs, and the legal and educational systems, covering the period of 1949-1969.

223. Liu, Alan P. L. *Political culture and group conflict in communist China.* Santa Barbara, CA : Clio Books, 1971. 205 p.
A study of the group conflicts in China from 1966 to 1969. Part one of the book gives a general view of the conflicts. Part two analyzes various parts of the conflicts, and examines the motivation and behavior of each conflicting group.

224. *Long live victory of the great cultural revolution under the dictatorship of the proletariat--in celebration of the 18th anniversary of the founding of the People's Republic of China.* Peking : Foreign Languages Press. 1968. 48 p.
Translation of: Wu chan jie ji zhuan zheng xia de wen hua da ge ming sheng li wan sui.
Includes Lin Biao and Zhou Enlai's speeches in celebrating the eighteenth anniversary of the founding of the People's Republic of China, and editorials of Renmin Ribao, Hongqi, and Jiefangjun Bao.

225. *Mao Tse-tung's thought is the invincible weapon.* Peking : Foreign Languages Press, 1968. 79 p.

226.   McCullough, Colin. *Stranger in China*. New York : Morrow, 1973. 292 p.
The author, as a correspondent, arrived in Beijing in the spring of 1968 with his wife and daughter. In this work, he presents a picture of life in Beijing during the period of 1968-1970.

227.   Mehnert, Klaus. *Peking and the new left : at home and abroad.* Berkeley : Center for Chinese studies, University of California, 1969. 156 p.
Explores the rise and fall of the ultra-left movement in China during the period of 1966-1969 including discussions and documents about the mass organizations "Sheng Wu Lian" and the "May 16 Corps."
Includes documents (p. 73-156).

228.   Oksenberg, Michel   et al. *Cultural revolution : 1967 in review : four essays.* Ann Arbor : University of Michigan, Center for Chinese Studies, 1968. 125 p.
Contains four essays covering China's foreign policy, economy, society, and structural changes during 1967.

229.   *On the proletarian revolutionaries' struggle to seize power*. Peking : Foreign Languages Press, 1967. 57 p.
Editorials from various newspapers and magazines.
Contents include: On the proletarian revolutionaries' struggle to seize power (Hongqi, no. 3, 1967); Proletarian revolutionaries form a great alliance to seize power from those in authority who are taking the capitalist road (Renmin Ribao, Jan. 22, 1967); The People's Liberation Army firmly backs the proletarian revolutionaries (Jiefangjun Bao, Jan. 25, 1967).

230.   *On the revolutionary "three-in-one" combination*. Peking : Foreign Languages Press, 1967. 37 p.
Translation of: Lun ge ming de san jie he, which was originally issued as an editorial of Hongqi on March 30, 1967.

231.   Pan Chao-ying. *Peking's Red Guards : the great proletarian cultural revolution*. New York : Twin Circle Publishing Co., 1968. 462 p.

232.   *People's China : social experimentation, politics entry into the world scene 1966 through 1972*. New York : Random House, 1974. 673 p.
Edited by David Milton and others.

233.   Possony, Stefan Thomas. *The revolution of madness*. Taipei : Institute of International Relations, 1971. 86 p.

234.   *Put Mao Tse-tung's thought in command of everything*. Peking : Foreign Languages Press, 1969. 19 p.
        It was issued as a New Year editorial for 1969 by Renmin Ribao, Hongqi, and Jiefangjun Bao.

235.   Qi Benyu. *Patriotism or national betrayal? On the reactionary film 'Inside Story of the Ching Court.'* Peking : Foreign Languages Press, 1967. 32 p.
        Translation of: Ai guo zhu yi hai shi mai guo zhu yi, an article criticizing Liu Shaoqi.

236.   *Red Guard publications = Hung wei ping tzu liao*. Washington, DC : Center for Chinese Research Materials, Association of Research Libraries, 1975-1979. 20 v. (6,743 p.).
        Text in Chinese with preface in Chinese and English. Reprinted from various newspapers, documents, and other materials.

237.   *Red Guard publications. Supplement = Hung wei ping tzu liao. Hsu pien*. Washington, DC : Center for Chinese Research Materials, Association of Research Libraries, 1980. 14 v.
        Supplement 1 (v.1-8); supplement 2 (v.1-8).
        Text in Chinese with English preface. Reprinted from various newspapers, documents, and other materials.

238.   Robinson, Joan. *The Cultural Revolution in China*. Harmondsworth, Middlesex, England ; Baltimore : Penguin Books, 1969. 151 p.
        Contains an introductory essay on the origins of the Cultural Revolution, a detailed account of the Cultural Revolution in Shanghai, and a selection of key Cultural Revolution documents.

239.   Robinson, Thomas W., ed. *Cultural revolution in China*. Berkeley : University of California Press, 1971. 509 p.
        Rand Corporation's studies on the early period of the Cultural Revolution. The five case studies cover subjects of ideology, policy-making, leadership, foreign policy, and the revolution in the countryside.

240.   Schoenhals, Michael, ed. *China's Cultural Revolution, 1966-1969 : not a dinner party*. Armonk, NY : M.E. Sharpe, 1996. 400 p.

Contains seventy-two primary documents issued mainly in the period of 1966-1969, which were selected from public and classified Chinese sources and translated into English.

241.   Schram, Stuart R., ed. *Authority, participation and cultural change in China*. New York : Cambridge University Press, 1973. 350 p.
Contains eight revised conference papers which were originally delivered at Urchfont Manor in September 1972. Discusses Chinese social, economic, education policies, familial and personal relationships, and other issues.

242.   Tong, Te-kong. *The uncultured cultural revolution in China : a background survey*. New York : Columbia University, University Seminar on Modern East Asia--China, 1966. 13 leaves.

243.   Tsao, James Jhy-yuan. *Chinese Communist Cultural Revolution : an analytical reappraisal from the historical point of view*. Thesis (Ph.D.). American University, 1974. 352 leaves.

244.   Wang Li, Jia Yixue, and Li Xin. *The dictatorship of the proletariat and the great proletarian cultural revolution*. Peking : Foreign Languages Press, 1967. 16 p.
Translation of: Wu chan jie ji zhuan zheng he wu chan jie ji wen hua da ge ming.

245.   Wang Li; Michael Schoenhals, ed. *An insider's account of the Cultural Revolution : Wang Li's memoirs*. Armonk, NY : M.E. Sharpe, 1994. 96 p.
Memoirs of Wang Li, who was the member of the CCP Central Cultural Revolution Group between 1966 and 1967.
It was published as Chinese Law and Government, vol. 27, no. 6.

246.   Wang Ming. *China : cultural revolution or counter-revolutionary coup?* Moscow : Novosti Press Agency Publishing House, 1969. 76 p.
Originally published in the Canadian Tribune on March 19, 1969.

247.   Weakland, John H. *Cultural aspects of China's "Cultural Revolution."* Palo Alto, CA : Mental Research Institute, 1969. 49 p.

248.   Yao Wenyuan. *Working class must exercise leadership in everything*. Peking : Foreign Languages Press, 1968. 20 p.
Translation of: Gong ren jie ji bi xu ling dao yi qie.

Original Chinese article published in the "Hongqi," no. 2, 1968.

249. Yeh Hsiang-chih. *The cause and effect of the "cultural revolution."* Taipei : World Anti-Communist League, 1970. 111 p.

250. Yeh Hsiang-chih. *Current situation in mainland China.* Taipei : Institute of International Relations, 1970. 1 v.

251. Yomiuri shimbun; Robert Trumbull, ed. *This is Communist China.* New York : McKay, 1968. 274 p.
An expansion and recasting of observations made by nine members of the Yomiuri task force who visited China in 1966.

252. Yu, Hen Mao. *Fishy winds and bloody rains.* Taipei : World Anti-Communist League, 1970. 89 p.

253. Zanegin, B. et al. *China and its cultural revolution : a Soviet analysis.* Washington, DC : Joint Publications Research Service, 1969. 53 p.

B. LIN BIAO AND THE LIN BIAO AFFAIR

254. An, Tai Sung. *The Lin Piao affair.* Philadelphia : Foreign Policy Research Institute in association with Lexington Books, 1974. 67 p.
In this monograph, author refuses to accept the Chinese official version, and attempts to reconstruct logically and analytically a possible chain of events surrounding the disappearance of Lin Biao.

255. Brosh, Charles L. *The end of the Chinese cultural revolution and the fall of Lin Piao : a study of the relationship of changing Chinese policies and the decline of Lin Piao, 1966-71.* Thesis (M.A.). Georgetown University, 1978. 497 leaves.

256. *Chairman Mao's successor : deputy supreme commander Lin Piao.* Washington, DC : reprinted by Center for Chinese Research Materials, Association of Research Libraries, 1970. 17, 24 leaves.
Text in Chinese and English. Title is also in Chinese: [Mao zhu xi de jie ban ren : Lin Biao fu tung shuai]. Chinese text originally published in China in June 1969. With an appended English translation produced by the American Consulate General in Hong Kong and originally published in Current Background, no. 894, October 27, 1969.

257. *Continue the revolution, advance from victory to victory.* Peking :
Foreign Languages Press, 1970. 17 p.
Consists of a speech by Lin Biao and a toast by Zhou Enlai at rallies held
in Beijing (Sept. 30 & Oct. 1, 1970), and an editorial from Renmin
Ribao, Hongqi and Jiefangjun Bao (Oct. 1, 1970).

258. Ebon, Martin. *Lin Piao : the life and writings of China's new ruler.*
New York : Stein and Day, 1970. 378 p.
Includes a brief biography of Lin Biao, and also contains twenty writings
written by Lin Biao during the period of 1940-1969.

259. Ginneken, Jaap van. *The rise and fall of Lin Piao.* New York : Avon
Books, 1977. 363 p.
Translation of: De linkse stroming in China.
Tracks Lin Biao's growing prominence after 1959. Analyzes the massive
upheaval of the Cultural Revolution, Lin Biao's role and activities in the
revolution, and events leading up to the fall of Lin Biao.

260. Hwang, Tien-chien. *Transformation of Mao-Lin faction's tactical line
for power seizure.* Taipei : Asian Peoples' Anti-Communist League,
1968. 94 p.

261. *Important documents on the great proletarian cultural revolution in
China.* Peking : Foreign Languages Press, 1970. 323 p.
It is substantially a collection of speeches by Lin Biao.

262. Kau, Michael Y. M., ed. *Lin Piao affair : power politics and military
coup.* White Plains, NY : International Arts and Sciences Press, 1975.
591 p.
Documents in this work are organized into five sections beginning with
a comprehensive biography of Lin Biao. About one half of the materials
are party documents, and the other half are from various Chinese
newspapers and journals. Also includes comprehensive collections of Lin
Biao's speeches, writings, messages and instructions from 1965 to 1970.

263. Li Tien-min. *The Mao-Lin relationship and Lin Piao's future.* Taipei :
Institute of International Relations, 1971. 40 p.

264. Lin Biao. *Quotations from Lin Piao.* Hong Kong : Chih Luen Press,
1971. 100 p.
Translation of: Lin Biao yu lu. Edited by China Problems Research
Center, Hong Kong.

265. Lin Biao. *Report to the ninth National Congress of the Communist Party of China (delivered on April 1 and adopted on April 14, 1969).* Peking : Foreign Languages Press, 1969. 105 p.

266. Lin Biao. *Selected works of Lin Piao.* Hong Kong : Chih Luen Press, 1970. 488 p.
Edited by China Problem Research Center, Hong Kong.

267. *Lin Piao : a Chinese Communist military leader.* Taipei : Office of Military History, 1971. 76 p.

268. Liu Yueh-sun. *Current and the past of Lin Piao.* Santa Monica, CA : Rand Corp., 1967. 58 p.
Translation of: Lin Biao de guo qu yu xian zai, originally published on the Studies on Chinese Communism, January 31, 1967.

269. Mao Zedong. *Mao Tse-tung and Lin Piao : post-revolutionary writings.* Garden City, NY : Doubleday, 1972. 536 p.
Contains writings of Mao Zedong and Lin Biao that have been written since 1949. The appendix includes two documents: the Decision of the Central Committee of the Chinese Communist Party concerning the Great Proletarian Cultural Revolution, and the Constitution of the Communist Party of China (adopted in 1969).

270. Powell, Ralph L. *Communist China : the increased influence of Lin Piao and the Armed Forces.* McLean, VA : Research Analysis Corporation, 1968. 54 p.

271. Robinson, Thomas W. *Lin Piao as an elite type.* Santa Monica, CA : Rand Corp., 1971. 56 p.

272. Robinson, Thomas W. *A political-military biography of Lin Biao.* Santa Monica, CA : Rand Corp., 1971. 2 v.
Contents include: Part I. 1907-1949. Part II, 1950-1971.

273. *Selected articles criticizing Lin Piao and Confucius.* Peking : Foreign Languages Press, 1974. 2 v.
Translation of articles originally published in Chinese.

274. *Summary of the forum on the work in literature and art in the armed forces with which comrade Lin Piao entrusted comrade Chiang Ching.* Peking : Foreign Languages Press, 1968. 48 p.

Translation of: Lin Biao tong zhi wei tuo Jiang Qing tong zhi zhao kai de bu dui wen yi gong zuo zuo tan hui ji yao.

275. Tao Lung-sheng. *Civil-military relations in China : Lin Piao and the PLA, 1959-1966.* Thesis (Ph.D.). University of Hawaii, Honolulu, 1971. 381 leaves.

276. Teiwes, Frederick C. and Warren Sun. *The tragedy of Lin Biao : riding the tiger during the Cultural Revolution, 1966-1971.* Honolulu : University of Hawaii Press, c1996. 251 p.
Offers an interpretation which undermines the standard view of Lin Biao as an ambitious politician to adopt a radical position during the Cultural Revolution. Reveals Lin Biao as someone basically uninterested in power and had no policy programmed. Lin Biao's political decline was due to Mao Zedong's reaction to complex factors unconnected with Lin Biao.

277. Weng Feng. *Lin Piao and his armed rebellion thinking.* Taipei : Asian Peoples' Anti-Communist League, 1967. 57 p.

278. Yao Mingle. *The conspiracy and death of Lin Biao.* 1st ed. New York : A.A. Knopf : Distributed by Random House, 1983. 231 p.
Focuses narrowly on the specific episode of the Lin Biao affair. The author's account of Lin Biao's death is different from the Chinese official version.

279. Yao Wenyuan. *On the social basis of the Lin Piao anti-party clique.* Peking : Foreign Languages Press, 1975. 28 p.
Translation of: Lun Lin Biao fan dang ji tuan de she hui ji chu.

280. Zhan Shipu. *Great victory for the military line of Chairman Mao Tsetung : a criticism of Lin Piao's bourgeois military line in the Liaohsi-Shenyang and Peiping-Tientsin campaigns.* Peking : Foreign Languages Press, 1976. 115 p.
Translation of: Mao zhu xi jun shi lu xian de wei da sheng li.

281. Zhang Yunsheng; Lawrence R. Sullivan, ed. *True account of Maojiawan : reminiscences of Lin Biao's secretary by Zhang Yunsheng.* Armonk, NY : M.E. Sharpe, 1993. 85 p.
It was published as Chinese law and government, vol. 27, no. 6. Translated from Chinese.

C. 1970-1976

282. *Advance victoriously along Chairman Mao's revolutionary line : 1971 New Year's day editorial.* Peking : Foreign Languages Press, 1971. 19 p.
An editorial of Renmin Ribao, Hongqi, and Jiefangjun Bao.

283. Barnett, A. Doak. *Uncertain passage : China's transition to the post-Mao era.* Washington, DC : Brookings Institution, 1974. 387 p.
Looks at the conflicts of values and problem of institutional stability in China. Analyzes the political roles and activities of the People's Liberation Army. Focuses on China's developmental problems, as well as the leadership and succession problems. Examines China's foreign policy.

284. Bloodworth, Dennis and Jingbing Bloodworth. *Heirs apparent : what happens when Mao dies?* New York : Straus, 1973. 236 p.
Highlights the personalities and political characteristics of the Chinese Communist leaders and their relationships with Mao Zedong, covering the period of 1920's to 1972.

285. Brugger, Bill, ed. *China : the impact of the cultural revolution.* New York : Barnes & Noble Books ; London : Croom Helm, 1978. 300 p.
Focuses on the period of 1969-1973 and includes the analysis of the role of the People's Liberation Army, revolution in education, strategy of economic development, two lines struggle in agriculture, industrial management, and foreign policy.

286. Central Intelligence Agency, U.S. *Bibliography of literature written in the People's Republic of China during the campaign to criticize Lin Piao and Confucius, July 1973-December 1974.* Washington, DC : Central Intelligence Agency, 1975. 220, 219 p.

287. Chan, Anita, Jonathan Unger, and Stanley Rosen, eds. *On socialist democracy and the Chinese legal system : the Li Yizhe debates.* Armonk, NY : M.E. Sharpe, 1985. 300 p.
A study of the Li-Yi-Zhe group from the 1970's to the early 1980's. Contains a translation of the famous wall post "On Socialist Democracy and the Chinese Legal System" and three other documents written by Li-Yi-Zhe group in Guangzhou in 1974. Also contains reports on their arrest, and the criticism towards them made by the Chinese authority.

288. Chi Hsin (Research Group). *The case of the Gang of Four*. Hong Kong : Cosmos Books Ltd., 1977. 295 p.
A collection of articles originally published on a Hong Kong magazine "The Seventies."

289. Chi Hsin (Research Group). *The case of the Gang of Four : with first translation of Teng Hsiao-ping's "Three poisonous weeds."* 2nd ed. Hong Kong : Cosmos Books, 1978. 314 p.

290. Chi Hsin (Research Group). *The rise and fall of the "Gang of Four" : some questions and answers.* New York : Books New China, 1977. 77 p.
Translated from an article originally appeared in the December 1976 issue of "The Seventies."

291. Chin, Steve S. K., ed. *Gang of Four : first essays after the fall : selected seminar papers on contemporary China, II.* Hong Kong : Centre of Asian Studies, University of Hong Kong, 1977. 191 p.

292. *Chinese communism in the 1970's.* Taipei : China Publishing Co., 1978. 209 p.
Includes eight papers presented to the 7th Sino-American Conference on Mainland China held in Taipei in 1978.

293. *Commemorate the 50th anniversary of the Communist Party of China.* Peking : China Reconstructs, 1971. 18 p.
An editorial of Renmin Ribao, Hongqi, and Jiefangjun Bao.

294. *Communists should be the advanced elements of the proletariat : in commemoration of the 49th anniversary of the founding of the Communist Party of China.* Peking : Foreign Languages Press, 1970. 12 p.

295. Derbyshire, Ian. *Politics in China from Mao to Deng.* Edinburgh : W. & R. Chambers, 1987. 134 p.
A summary of Chinese political history since 1949 with particular attention to the changes between 1972 and 1987.

296. Domes, Jurgen. *China after the Cultural Revolution : politics between two party congresses.* London : C. Hurst, 1976. 283 p.
An analysis of Chinese politics between 1969 and 1973. Translation of: China nach der Kulturrevolution : Politik zwischen zwei Partenitagen.

297. Domes, Jurgen. *China after the Cultural Revolution : politics between two party congresses.* 1st American ed. Berkeley : University of California Press, 1977. 283 p.

298. Dunayevskaya, Raya. *Sexism, politics and revolution in Mao's China.* Detroit, MI : Women's Liberation, News and Letters Committees, 1977. 19 p.
      Contents include: Chiang Ch'ing, Hua Kuo-feng in post-Mao China; Alienation and revolution, a Hong Kong interview.

299. *Eternal glory to the great leader and teacher Chairman Mao Tsetung.* Peking : Foreign Languages Press, 1976. 40 p.
      Contents include: Message to the whole party, the whole army, and the people of all nationalities throughout the country; Memorial speech; Decision on the establishment of a memorial hall for the great leader and teacher Chairman Mao Testing.

300. Fenwick, Ann Elizabeth. *The Gang of Four and the politics of opposition : China, 1971-1976.* Thesis (Ph.D.). Stanford University, 1983. 599 leaves.

301. Fingar, Thomas and Paul Blencowe, eds. *China's quest for independence : policy evolution in the 1970's.* Boulder, CO : Westview Press, 1980. 256 p.
      Examines the policies development in the 1970s. Traces the evolution of policies on specific issues such as education, foreign trade, and military.

302. Gates, Millicent Anne and E. Bruce Geelhoed. *The dragon and the snake : an American account of the turmoil in China, 1976-1977.* Philadelphia : University of Pennsylvania Press, 1986. 222 p.
      Gives accounts of those events from the perspective of an American official stationed in China. Provides a firsthand view of the power struggle between rival political factions, the earthquakes, the arrest of the Gang of Four, and the Deng Xiaoping's return to leadership in mid-1977.

303. *Great historic victory : in warm celebration of Chairman Hua Kuo-feng's becoming leader of the Communist Party of China, and of the crushing of the Wang-Chang-Chiang-Yao anti-party clique.* Peking : Foreign Languages Press, 1976. 44 p.
      Translation of "Wei da de li shi xing sheng li," an editorial of Renmin Ribao, Hongqi, Jiefangjun Bao, October 25, 1976.

304. *Great leader Chairman Mao will live forever in our hearts.* Peking : s.n., 1976. 65 p.
On back cover: September 20, 1976.

305. Isenberg, Irwin, comp. *China : new force in world affairs.* New York : Wilson, 1972. 219 p.
A compilation of articles presenting various points of view on contemporary life and government policy in China.

306. Jain, Jagdish P. *After Mao what? Army, party and group rivalries in China.* Boulder, CO : Westview Press, 1976. 276 p.
Seeks to identify various group rivalries which might play significant roles in determining Chinese leadership.

307. Lau, Yee-fui. *Book and magazine bibliography of the "Criticise Lin Piao, Criticise Confucius" campaign.* Hong Kong : Universities Service Centre, [197-]. 14 p.

308. Lotta, Raymond, ed. *And Mao makes 5 : Mao Tse-tung's last great battle.* Chicago : Banner Press, 1978. 522 p.
Examines the power struggle at the top of the Chinese Communist Party in the period of 1973-1976.

309. Louie, Kam. *Critiques of Confucius in contemporary China.* New York : St. Martin's Press, 1980. 186 p.

310. Mao Zedong. *People of the world, unite and defeat the U.S. aggressors and all their running dogs : statement of May 20, 1970.* Peking : Foreign Languages Press, 1970. 8 p.

311. Meng Te-Sheng. *The anti-Confucian movement in the People's Republic of China, 1966-1974.* Thesis (Ph.D.). St. John's University, 1980. 221 leaves.

312. Meng Te-Sheng. *Chinese communism vs. Confucianism (1966-1974) : an historical and critical study.* New York : Free Men Magazine, 1980. 219 p.

313. Payne, Robert. *A rage for China.* New York : Holt, 1977. 276 p.
A description of major events in 1976-77, the denunciations of Jiang Qing and the Gang of Four on posts, newspapers, and in meetings.

314. *Report on China.* Peking : China Features, 1973. 126 p.

315. *Selected articles criticizing Lin Piao and Confucius.* Peking : Foreign Languages Press, 1974. 2 v.
A collection of articles by various authors that appeared previously in Chinese newspapers and periodicals.

316. *Selected essays on the study of philosophy by workers, peasants, and soldiers.* Peking : Foreign Languages Press, 1971. 83 p.

317. Sidel, Ruth. *Revolutionary China : people, politics and ping-pong.* New York : Delacorte Press, 1974. 178 p.
A personal view of China in light of its past history and present day aspirations.

318. *Strive for new victories : in celebration of the 23rd anniversary of the founding of the People's Republic of China, editorial [of Renmin Ribao, Hongqi, Jiefangjun Bao].* Peking : Foreign Languages Press, 1972. 11 p.

319. *United to win still greater victories.* Peking : Foreign Languages Press, 1972. 13 p.
Translation of: Tuan jie qi lai, zheng qu geng da de sheng li, which was issued as a New Year's editorial for 1972 by Renmin Ribao, Hongqi, and Jiefangjun Bao.

320. *Usher in the great 1970's : 1970 New Year's Day editorial of Renmin Ribao, Hongqi and Jiefangjun Bao.* Peking : Foreign Languages Press, 1970. 19 p.

321. Wong, Paul. *China's higher leadership in the socialist transition.* New York : Free Press, 1976. 316 p.

322. *Workers, peasants and solders criticize Lin Piao and Confucius : a collection of articles.* Peking : Foreign Languages Press, 1976. 108 p.

323. Wu Tien-wei. *Lin Biao and the Gang of Four : counter-Confucianism in historical and intellectual perspective.* Carbondale : Southern Illinois University Press, c1983. 283 p.
Examines the Chinese intellectual development in the 1970s with focus on the Criticizing of Lin Biao and Confucius movement and the campaign against the Gang of Four.

324. Yang Rongguo. *Confucius, "Sage" of the reactionary classes.* Peking : Foreign Languages Press, 1974. 66 p.
Translation of: Fan dong jie ji de sheng ren: Kongzi.

325. Zhang Chunqiao. *On exercising all-round dictatorship over the bourgeoisie.* Peking : Foreign Languages Press, 1975. 25 p.
Translation of an article "Lun dui zi chan jie ji de quan mian zhuan zheng," which was originally published in Hongqi, no. 4, 1975.

D. TRIAL OF LIN BIAO AND THE GANG OF FOUR CLIQUES

326. Bonavia, David. *Verdict in Peking : the trial of the Gang of Four.* London : Burnett, 1984. 225 p.
Includes transcripts from the Chinese TV broadcasts of excerpts from the trial (1980-1981).

327. *Great trial in Chinese history : the trial of the Lin Biao and Jiang Qing counter-revolutionary cliques, Nov. 1980-Jan. 1981.* 1st ed. Beijing, China : New World Press ; Elmsford, NY : Distribution by Pergamon Press, 1981. 234 p.
A Chinese official report of the trial of Lin Biao and the Gang of Four cliques.

328. *Indictment against Lin Biao-Jiang Qing cliques.* Hong Kong : Ta Kung Pao (English Supplement), 1980. 38 p.
Document was issued by the Special Prosecutor, the People's Republic of China.

IV

Cultural Revolution in Provinces and Municipalities

329. Central Intelligence Agency, U.S. *China city briefs*. Washington, DC : U.S. Government Printing Office, 1975. 167 p.
Gives descriptive information on thirteen Chinese cities: Anshan, Changsha, Zhengzhou, Chongqing, Hangzhou, Guangzhou, Guilin, Kunming, Beijing, Shanghai, Suzhou, Tianjin, and Wuhan.

330. Chiang, Chiahsiung. *The CCP provincial party first secretary : recruitment and career, 1949-1987*. Thesis (Ph.D.). Michigan State University, 1990. 262 leaves.

331. *China's provincial statistics, 1949-1989*. Boulder, CO : Westview Press, 1993. 595 p.
Edited by Hsueh Tien-tung, Li Qiang, Liu Shucheng.
Contents: Pt. 1. Provincial statistics. Pt. 2. Exposition of the key variables. Includes English-Chinese indexes of key variables.

332. *Cultural revolution in the provinces*. Cambridge, MA : East Asian Research Center, Harvard University; distributed by Harvard University Press, 1971. 216 p.
Four case studies by M. Sargent and others, focus on the Cultural Revolution in Heilongjiang, Shanghai, Sichuan, and Wuhan, being revisions of papers originally prepared for a seminar on Chinese Communist Society held in the spring of 1970 at Harvard University.

333.   Emerson, John Philip et al. *Provinces of the People's Republic of China : a political and economic bibliography.* Washington, DC : U.S. Department of Commerce, Bureau of Economic Analysis, 1976. 734 p.
This bibliography consists of over 6,000 citations of sources of data and information on the political and economic developments at the provincial level in China.

334.   Endicott, Stephen Lyon. *Red earth : revolution in a Sichuan village.* London : I. Tauris, 1988. 261 p.
A description of the changes that had taken place in the countryside since 1949. Based upon interviews as well as Chinese government documents, local records, and newspapers, it reveals through microcosm of village life the dynamics of China's revolutionary social, economic, and cultural transformation.

335.   Forster, Keith. *The Hangzhou Incident of 1975 : the impact of factionalism on a Chinese provincial administration.* Thesis (Ph.D.). University of Adelaide, 1985. 366 p.

336.   Forster, Keith. *Rebellion and factionalism in a Chinese province : Zhejiang, 1966-1976.* Armonk, NY : M.E. Sharpe, c1990. 338 p.
A detailed analysis of events in Zhejiang Province during the Cultural Revolution. Describes and analyzes the nature and composition of the mass organizations. Also investigates the links between prominent personnel of the mass organizations and provincial/central civilian and military party leaders.

337.   Goodman, David S. G. *China's provincial leaders, 1949-1985.* Atlantic Highlands, NJ : Humanities Press International, 1986-1987. 3 v.
Identifies individuals and their positions held by provincial and regional level unit, from 1949 till 1985.
Vol. 1 is a directory identifying the leaders by province or region. Vols. 2 and 3 provide detailed biographies.

338.   Gray, Sherry. *Bombard the headquarters : local politics and citizen participation in the Great Proletarian Cultural Revolution and the 1989 Movement in Shenyang.* Thesis (Ph.D.). University of Denver, Graduate School of International Studies, 1992. 429 leaves.

339.   *Great Tangshan earthquake.* Pasadena, CA : California Institute of Technology, 1996- (v. 1 & 4 published).
Edited by Xie Li-li.

340. *Great victory for Chairman Mao's revolutionary line : warmly hail the birth of Peking Municipal Revolutionary Committee.* Peking : Foreign Languages Press, 1967. 88 p.
A collection of speeches by Zhou Enlai, Jiang Qing, Xie Fuzhi and others, together with editorials from Renmin Ribao, Jiefangjun Bao, and Hongqi on the establishment of the Beijing Municipal Revolutionary Committee, April 20, 1967.

341. Howe, Christopher, ed. *Shanghai : revolution and development in an Asian metropolis.* Cambridge, England : Cambridge University Press, 1980. 456 p.
A collection of essays covering political, economical, cultural and other subject areas about Shanghai between 1949 and late 1970s.

342. Hunter, Neale. *Shanghai journal : an eyewitness account of the Cultural Revolution.* Hong Kong ; New York : Oxford University Press, 1988. 311 p.
A personal eyewitness account of the Cultural Revolution in Shanghai from 1966 to 1967. With a new introduction by the author. Originally published by Praeger Publishers in 1969.

343. Knight, Sophia. *Window on Shanghai : letters from China, 1965-67.* London : Andre Deutsch, 1967. 256 p.
The author was in Shanghai to teach English in the period of 1965-1967. In a series of letters to her mother, she describes what she saw in the streets, at meetings, on her traveling holidays, and in the Foreign Languages Institute where she was working.

344. Kruze, Uldis. *Political reconstitution of Peking Municipality : politics and polemics of the Cultural Revolution.* Thesis (Ph.D.). Indiana University, 1976. 344 leaves.

345. MacKerras, Colin and Neale Hunter. *China Observed : 1964-1967.* London : Pall Mall Press, 1968. 194 p.
Authors as English teachers in Shanghai provide an inside view of the Cultural Revolution in the city of Shanghai covering the period of 1966-1967.

346. Martin, Charles Michael. *Red Guards and political institutions : a study of Peking and Canton.* Thesis (Ph.D.). Harvard University, 1975. 525 leaves.

347. McMillan, Donald Hugh. *Chinese Communist power and policy in Xinjiang, 1945-1977*. Boulder, CO : Westview Press, 1979. 383 p.
A detailed study of the history of Xinjiang Uygur Autonomous Region. The degree of similarity and difference between the power and policy perspectives of the regional leadership and those of the central authorities in Beijing from 1949 to 1977 is a central concern of this book. Contents include "Part 4: The Cultural Revolution in Xinjiang, 1966-69" and "Part 5: Power and policy in Xinjiang after Wang Enmao, 1969-77."

348. Mehnert, Klaus. *Peking and the new left : at home and abroad*. Berkeley : Center for Chinese Studies, University of California, 1969. 156 p.
A study of a mass organization in Hunan Province--the Hunan Provincial Proletarian Revolution Great Alliance Committee.

349. Napier, Mark D. *Gang of Four and Shanghai : a study of three campaigns*. Nathan, Qld., Australia : School of Modern Asian Studies, Griffith University, 1984. 57 p.

350. Perry, Elizabeth J. and Li Xun. *Proletarian power : Shanghai in the Cultural Revolution*. Boulder, CO : Westview Press, 1996. 249 p.
Offers an in-depth study of Chinese labor activism in Shanghai during the Cultural Revolution. Explores three distinctive and different forms of working-class protest: rebellion, conservatism, and economism. And examines the divergent political, psychocultural, and socioeconomic strains within the Shanghai labor movement.

351. *Precarious balance : Hong Kong between China and Britain, 1842-1992*. Armonk, NY : M.E. Sharpe, 1994. 235 p.
Edited by Ming K. Chan, with the collaboration of John D. Young. Chapters 8 & 9 focus on the periods of 1950-1971 and 1971-1986.

352. Raddock, David M. *Political behavior of adolescents in China : the cultural revolution in Kwangchow*. Tuscon, AZ : Published for the Association for Asian Studies by the University of Arizona Press, 1977. 242 p.

353. Robinson, Thomas W. *The Wuhan incident : local strife and provincial rebellion during the Cultural Revolution*. Santa Monica, CA : Rand Corp., 1970. 32 leaves.
A quite detailed account of the Wuhan Incident in July and August 1967.

354. Rosen, Stanley. *Red Guard factionalism and the Cultural Revolution in Guangzhou (Canton)*. Boulder, CO : Westview Press, 1982. 320 p.
Studies the reasons behind the division of students into two large factions during the Cultural Revolution in Guangzhou. Analyzes internal divisions within the faction and subfactions showing the social bases for membership. Focuses on middle school students, but looks also at some university students.

355. Sweeney, Nancy Winston. *The Hong Kong disturbances and the Cultural Revolution, 1967*. Thesis (M.A.). Miami University, 1981. 102 leaves.

356. Teiwes, Frederick C. *Provincial leadership in China : the cultural revolution and its aftermath*. Ithaca, NY : Cornell University, 1974. 165 p.
Analyzes the changes in Chinese provincial personnel from 1967 to 1973.

357. Terrill, Ross. *Flowers on an iron tree : five cities of China*. Boston : Little, Brown, 1975. 423 p.
Describes five Chinese cities: Shanghai, Dalian, Hangzhou, Wuhan, and Beijing.

358. Unger, Jonathan. *Education under Mao : class and competition in Canton schools, 1960-1980*. New York : Columbia University Press, 1982. 308 p.
Examines and analyzes the changes or strategies of the 1960s, and the changes in job allocations, labor participation, course content, and peer group activities during the 1970s.

359. Vogel, Ezra F. *Canton under communism program and politics in a provincial capital, 1949-1968*. Cambridge, MA : Harvard University Press, 1969. 448 p.

360. Walder, Andrew George. *Chang Ch'un-chiao and Shanghai's January Revolution*. Ann Arbor : Center for Chinese Studies, University of Michigan, 1978. 150 p.
Provides an interpretation of Shanghai's January Revolution in 1967 and Zhang Chunqiao's role in this event.

361. Wang Shaoguang. *Failure of charisma : the Cultural Revolution in Wuhan*. Hong Kong ; New York : Oxford University Press, 1995. 345 p.

A study to provide an in-depth analysis of micro-politics in Wuhan from 1966 to 1976, and to examine the theoretical implications of mass behavior there based upon archival data, personal interviews with more than 85 former political activists including well-known factional leaders, and correspondence.

362. Watson, Andrew. *The cultural revolution in Sian.* Adelaide, Australia : Center for Asian Studies, University of Adelaide, 1967. 31 p.
Articles reprinted from: the Far Eastern Economic Review, 1967. vol. LVI, no. 3-5, 7-8; vol. LVII, no. 8.

363. White, Lynn T. *Shanghai's policy in Cultural Revolution.* [S.l. : s.n.], 1969. 65, 10 leaves.
Articles are prepared for *The city in communist China,* edited by G. William Skinner and John Wilson Lewis.

364. Woody, W.; Michael Schoenhals, ed. *The Cultural Revolution in Inner Mongolia : extracts from an unpublished history.* Stockholm : Center for Pacific Asia Studies at Stockholm University, 1993. 35 p.

365. Zheng Yi; T. P. Sym, ed. *Scarlet memorial : tales of cannibalism in modern China.* Boulder, CO : Westview Press, 1996. 199 p.
Translation of: Hong se ji nian bei.
Provides documented account of events in Guangxi during the Cultural Revolution. It is drawing on the author's unique access to local archives of the Chinese Communist Party and on extensive interviews with local officials, the victims' relatives, and the murderers themselves.

V

Special Subjects

A. MILITARY

366. Bullard, Monte R. *China's political military evolution : the party and the military in the People's Republic of China, 1960-1984.* Boulder, CO : Westview Press, 1985. 209 p.
Studies the structural change in China during the period of 1960-1984 by looking at institutional linkage in the political-military relationship.

367. Chien Yu-shen. *China's fading revolution : army dissent and military divisions, 1967-68.* Hong Kong : Centre of Contemporary Chinese Studies, 1969. 405 p.
Examines the events which unfolded after the Wuhan Incident in July-August 1967, and discusses the relationships between the regional military commanders and the central authorities in Beijing. Includes very useful documentary appendixes, as well as glossary, bibliography, and index.

368. Ching Shui-hsien. *Rifle rectifies rifle in Mao's cultural revolution.* Taipei : Asian Peoples' Anti-Communist League, 1969. 4, 75, 4 p.
Examines the role of the People's Liberation Army as an instrument of rectification before and during the Cultural Revolution.

369. Chu Wen-lin. *Personnel changes in the military regions and districts before and after the cultural revolution.* Taipei : Institute of International Relations, 1971. 54 p.

370. Chunlachip Chinawanno. *The militia in Chinese politics : 1949-1976.* Thesis (Ph.D.). Stanford University, 1981. 221 leaves.

371. Corr, Gerard H. *The Chinese Red Army : campaigns and politics since 1949.* Reading, Berkshire : Osprey Publishing, 1974. 175 p.

372. Defense Intelligence Agency, U.S. *Chinese armed forces today : the U.S. Defense Intelligence Agency handbook of China's army, navy, and air force.* 1st American ed. Englewood Cliffs, NJ : Prentice-Hall, 1979. 240 p.
      Includes information on Chinese military tactics, organization, etc. It was first published in 1976 under the title: *Handbook on the Chinese armed forces.*

373. *Fifty years of the Chinese People's Liberation Army.* Peking : Foreign Languages Press, 1978. 175 p.

374. Fraser, Angus M. *The changing role of the PLA under the impact of the cultural revolution.* Arlington, VA : Institute for Defense Analyzes International and Social Studies Division, 1969. 100 p.

375. Fraser, Angus M. *The People's Liberation Army : communist China's armed forces.* New York : Grane, Russak, 1973. 62 p.

376. Jencks, Harlan W. *From muskets to missiles : politics and professionalism in the Chinese army, 1945-1981.* Boulder, CO : Westview Press, 1982. 322 p.
      Provides a detailed description and evaluation of the military, political, economic, and social context within which People's Liberation Army officers functioned in the period of 1945-1981. Several sections including Chapter IV "Professionalism on trial" focus on the People's Liberation Army's roles and activities during the Cultural Revolution.

377. Jencks, Harlan W. *The politics of Chinese military development, 1945-1977.* Thesis (Ph.D.). University of Washington at Seattle, 1978. 2 v.

378. Kau, Michael Y. M. *The People's Liberation Army and China's nation-building.* White Plains, NY : International Arts and Sciences Press, 1973. 407 p.
      This study is to present, in the Chinese leadership's own words and conceptualization, the Chinese model of army-building and its contributions to the Chinese political development and socioeconomic

modernization of China. Thirty-two documents and writings were selected for this book. The last part (sections VI-VIII) emphasizes the operational dynamics of the model since 1949.

379. Lee, Luke Wen-yuen. *Role of the military in Mainland China's power struggles : 1966-1969*. Thesis (Ph.D.). University of Idaho, 1975. 170 leaves.

380. Nelsen, Harvey W. *The Chinese military system : an organizational study of the Chinese People's Liberation Army*. Boulder, CO : Westview Press, 1977. 266 p.
Studies the Chinese military system mainly from the eve of the Cultural Revolution to mid-1976.

381. Nelsen, Harvey W. *The Chinese military system : an organizational study of the Chinese People's Liberation Army*. 2nd ed. (revised and updated). Boulder, CO : Westview Press, 1981. 285 p.
This second edition has been revised to reflect changes that occurred since the death of Mao Zedong (1976) as well as to incorporate new information about Chinese military and political system during Mao's era.

382. Nelsen, Harvey W. *An organizational history of the Chinese People's Liberation Army, 1966-1969*. Thesis (Ph.D.). George Washington University, 1972. 278 leaves.

383. Wang, James C. F. *The People's Liberation Army in Communist China's political development : a contingency analysis of the military's perception and verbal symbolization during the Cultural Revolution, 1966-1969*. Thesis (Ph.D.). University of Hawaii, Honolulu, 1971. 282 leaves.

384. Wang, Shu-shin. *Party army relationship in the People's Republic of China, 1959-1977*. Thesis (Ph.D.). West Virginia University, 1977. 527 leaves.

385. Whitson, William W. *The Chinese communist high command : a history of military politics, 1927-69*. New York ; London : Praeger Publishers, 1971. 638 p.
Chapters 7 and 8 are devoted to a study of the role and activities of the Chinese military leaders in the Cultural Revolution.

386. Whitson, William W. *The Chinese high command, a history of communist military politics, 1927-1971*. New York : Praeger Publishers, 1973. 557 p.
   Chapters 7 and 8 are devoted to a study of the role and activities of the People's Liberation Army leaders in the Cultural Revolution (1965-1970).

387. Whitson, William W. *The distribution of power among military and civil interest groups in China, 1956-1971*. Santa Monica, CA : Rand Corp., 1973. 31 p.

388. Whitson, William W., ed. *Military and political power in China in the 1970s*. New York : Praeger Publishers, 1972. 390 p.
   Focuses on the military's role in Chinese politics, the involvement during the Cultural Revolution, the power of the professional commanders, the organization of military power, and Chinese military strategies and tactics.

389. Zhu Fang. *Party-army relations in Maoist China, 1949-1976*. Thesis (Ph.D.). Columbia University, 1994. 435 leaves.

B. EDUCATION AND CULTURE

390. Alley, Rewi. *Building a socialist educational system in China : China's Cultural Revolution in education*. New York : Maud Russell Publisher, 1974. 63 p.

391. Barlow, Tani E. and Donald M. Lowe. *Teaching China's lost generation : foreign experts in the People's Republic of China*. San Francisco : China Books & Periodicals, 1987. 267 p.

392. Bietz, Gray Roy. *The politics of educational reform in the People's Republic of China : revolutionary destruction, 1966-1968*. Thesis (Ph.D.). New York University, 1972. 334 leaves.

393. Blumenthal, Eileen Polley. *Models in Chinese moral education : perspectives from children's books*. Thesis (Doctoral). University of Michigan, 1976. 242 leaves.

394. Bratton, Dale Lester. *The politics of educational reform in the People's Republic of China, 1966-1973*. Thesis (Ph.D.). University of California, Berkeley. 1978. 311 leaves.

395. Chen, Theodore Hsi-en. *Chinese education since 1949 : academic and revolutionary models*. New York : Pergamon Press. 1981. 249 p.
Examines the changes in contemporary Chinese education from the standpoint of shifts and swings between two contrasting models of education. The education revolution and the revolutionary model of education that emerged from it are the topics of chapters 6 and 7.

396. Chen, Theodore Hsi-en. *The Maoist educational revolution*. New York : Praeger Publishers. 1974. 295 p.

397. Fraser, Stewart E. and Kuang-liang Hsu. *Chinese education and society : a bibliographic guide : the cultural revolution and its aftermath*. White Plains, NY : International Arts and Sciences Press. 1972. 204 p.

398. Gregory, Peter B. and Noele Krenkel. *China : education since the Cultural Revolution : selected, partially annotated bibliography of English translations*. San Francisco : Evaluation and Research Analysts. 1972. 1 v.

399. Hawkins, John N. *Education and social change in the People's Republic of China*. New York : Praeger Publishers. 1983. 237 p.

400. Hawkins, John N. *The educational thought of Mao Tse-tung*. Thesis (Ph.D.). George Peabody College for Teachers. 1973. 279 leaves.

401. Hinton, William. *Hundred day war : the cultural revolution at Tsinghua University*. New York : Monthly Review Press 1972. 288 p.
A study of the Cultural Revolution as it occurred on the campus of Tsinghua (Qinghua) University which took a leading role in the Red Guard movement. The author spent seven months in China in 1971 and interviewed some of the participants about their involvement in the revolution.

402. Hsu, Kuang-liang. *Chinese communist education : the Cultural Revolution and aftermath*. Thesis (Ph.D.). George Peabody College for Teachers. 1972. 535 leaves.

403. Hu, Shi Ming and Eli Seifman, eds. *Toward a new world outlook : a documentary history of education in the People's Republic of China, 1949-1976.* New York : AMS Press, 1976. 335 p.
A documentary survey of educational policies and trends over the period of 1949-1976.

404. Kan, David. *The impact of the Cultural Revolution on Chinese higher education.* Kowloon : Union Research Institute, 1971. 183 p.

405. Kessen, William, ed. *Childhood in China : American Delegation on Early Childhood Development in the People's Republic of China.* New Haven, CT : Yale University Press, 1975. 241 p.
It is a report of an American delegation that visited China in 1973 to study child rearing and early education. The delegation visited nurseries, kindergartens, schools, hospitals, clinics, the Shanghai Youth Palace, and discussed with educationists, officials, parents, teachers, doctors, and Little Red Guards.

406. Kwong, Julia. *Chinese education in transition : prelude to the Cultural Revolution.* Montreal : McGill-Queen's University Press, c1979. 207 p.
Focuses on the conflicts over Chinese education policy. Analyzes the Chinese education in its social context and traces the reforms on education back to the continuation of class struggle in Chinese society. It is based on both English and Chinese sources, supplemented by interviews from visitors to China.

407. Kwong, Julia. *Cultural revolution in China's schools, May 1966-April 1969.* Stanford, CA : Hoover Institution Press, c1988. 200 p.

408. Lin Yanzi. *Mao Zedong's philosophy of adult education.* Thesis (Ed.D.). Northern Illinois University, 1989. 257 leaves.

409. Liu Liping. *Gains and loses : five teachers perspectives on their cultural revolution educational experiences and current teaching philosophy.* Thesis (Ed.D.). Harvard Graduate School of Education, 1997. 185 leaves.

410. Lofstedt, Jan-Ingvar. *Chinese education policy : changes and contradictions, 1949-1979.* Stockholm : Almqvist & Wiksell International, 1980. 203 p.

411. Nee, Victor, with Don Layman. *The cultural revolution at Peking University.* New York : Monthly Review Press, c1969. 91 p.
A detailed chronological account of the upheaval in the Peking University, 1965-1966. The appendix includes articles from Red Guard newspapers.

412. Pepper, Suzanne. *Radicalism and education reform in 20th-century China : the search for an ideal development model.* Cambridge, England ; New York : Cambridge University Press, 1996. 610 p.
The study of both pre-1949 and post-1949 China provides the historical perspective on Chinese education reform. The author uses four to five sections to cover China's educational experience in the Cultural Revolution period.

413. Price, R. F. *Education in modern China.* [2nd ed.]. London ; Boston : Routledge & Kegan Paul, 1979. 344 p.
Originally published: *Education in Communist China.* New York : Praeger Publishers, 1970. 308 p.
Analyzes Mao Zedong's thoughts, shows how the Chinese educational policies have had to face the inertia of pre-World War II schools strongly influenced by foreign practice, and gives detailed accounts of the full and part-time systems of education. Also introduces the major events in education which followed the death of Mao Zedong in 1976.

414. Proett, Polly-Ann Brumley. *A history of libraries in the People's Republic of China, including some aspects of college and university library development, 1949-1974.* Thesis (Ed.D.). George Washington University, 1974. 231 leaves.

415. Seeberg, Vilma. *Literacy in China : the effect of the national development context and policy on literacy levels, 1949-1979.* Bochum, Germany : Brockmeyer, 1990. 352 p.
Studies the relationship between background elements, human resource development policy, and educational attainment at the level of literacy in China. Examines the factors including cultural, socio-economic, educational policy, schooling quality and content factors, and their interactive effect firstly on participation in education and secondly on educational attainment patterns in the population.

416. Seybolt, Peter J., comp. *Revolutionary education in China.* White Plains, NY : International Arts & Sciences Press, 1973. 408 p.

Materials translated were first published in the Chinese press. Five topics are discussed in the book: broad objectives; conditions affecting educational theory and practice; the struggle between two lines; events of the early years of Cultural Revolution; educational principles which were applied in 1970's.

417.   Sherman, James C. *Mao Tse-tung's concept of higher education*. Thesis (Ph.D.). University of Denver, Colorado, 1972. 177 leaves.

418.   Shockro, Ellen Krosney. *The effects of the Cultural Revolutionary experiment on teachers and teaching in the People's Republic of China 1966-1973*. Thesis (Ph.D.). Claremont Graduate School, 1980. 172 leaves.

419.   *Strive to build a socialist university of science and engineering*. Peking : Foreign Languages Press, 1972. 69 p.
Includes essays: "Workers' and People's Liberation Army men's Mao Tsetung Thought Propaganda Team at Tsinghua University. Strive to build a socialist university of science and engineering," and "Summary of the Forum on the Revolution in Education in Shanghai College of Science and Engineering."

420.   *Take the road of the Shanghai Machine Tools Plant in training technicians from among the workers : two investigation reports on the revolution in education in colleges of science and engineering*. Peking : Foreign Languages Press, 1968. 56 p.
Consists of two articles regarding the experiments on technical education in Shanghai during the Cultural Revolution.

421.   Teng Ssu-yu. *Education and intellectual life in China after the cultural revolution*. Bloomington, IN : East Asian Studies Program, Indiana University, 1972. 16 leaves.

422.   Unger, Jonathan. *Education under Mao : class and competition in Canton schools, 1960-1980*. New York : Columbia University Press, 1982. 308 p.
Examines and analyzes the changes or strategies of the 1960s, and the changes in job allocations, labor participation, course content, and peer group activities during the 1970s.

423. Wang Hsueh-wen. *Higher education on China Mainland since cultural revolution*. Taipei : World Anti-Communist League, 1980. 119 p.

424. Weakland, John H. *Cultural aspects of China's "Cultural Revolution."* Palo Alto, CA : Mental Research Institute, 1969. 49 p.

425. Yin Chih-peng. *The cultural revolution in Chinese higher education : the mass line*. Thesis (Ph.D.). Columbia University, 1973. 139 leaves.

C. YOUTH, WOMEN, AND INTELLECTUALS

426. Andors, Phyllis. *The unfinished liberation of Chinese women, 1949-1980*. Bloomington : Indiana University Press, c1983. 224 p.
Describes the political, economic, and social experiences of rural and urban Chinese women.

427. Bernstein, Thomas P. *Up to the mountains and down to the villages : the transfer of youth from urban to rural China*. New Haven, CT : Yale University Press, 1977. 371 p.
An analysis of China's actions to resettle urban youth in countryside in the early 1970s.

428. Chan, Anita. *Children of Mao : personality development and political activism in the Red Guard generation*. Seattle, WA : University of Washington Press, c1985. 254 p.
Studies the inner world of young Chinese growing up in the Cultural Revolution based upon interviews held in Hong Kong. Contains four case studies.

429. Chan, Che-po. *From idealism to pragmatism : the change of political thinking among the Red Guard generation in China*. Thesis (Ph.D.). University of California, Santa Barbara, 1991. 295 leaves.

430. Croll, Elisabeth, ed. *Women's movement in China : a selection of readings, 1949-1973*. London : Anglo-Chinese Educational Institute, 1974. 115 p.

431. Goldman, Merle. *China's intellectuals : advice and dissent*. Cambridge, MA : Harvard University Press, 1981. 276 p.

A study of the writers, philosophers, historians, journalists, and scientists in China, to analyze the cultural aspects of the Cultural Revolution covering the entire decade from 1966 to 1976.

432.   Goldman, Merle, with Timothy Cheek and Carol Lee Hamrin, eds. *China's intellectuals and the state : in search of a new relationship.* Cambridge, MA : Council on East Asian Studies, Harvard University ; Distributed by the Harvard University Press, 1987. 374 p.
Group studies of economists, lawyers, professionals, scientists, writers, and others in China. Focuses mainly on the post-Mao period, but also deals with connections with the Mao's era including the Cultural Revolution period.

433.   Gregory, Peter B. and Noele Krenkel. *China : education since the Cultural Revolution : selected, partially annotated bibliography of English translations.* San Francisco : Evaluation and Research Analysts, 1972. 1 v.

434.   Grieder, Jerome B. *Intellectuals and the state in modern China : a narrative history.* New York : Free Press ; London : Collier Macmillian, 1981. 395 p.

435.   Hamrin, Carol Lee and Timothy Cheek, eds. *China's establishment intellectuals.* Armonk, NY : M.E. Sharpe, 1986. 266 p.
Focuses on the reactions of China's intellectual establishment to the failures of the Great Leap Forward (1958-1960) and the roles of these intellectuals in the Cultural Revolution.

436.   Hemmel, Vibeke and Pia Sindbjerg. *Women in rural China : policy towards women before and after the Cultural Revolution.* London : Curzon Press ; Atlantic Highlands, NJ : Humanities Press, 1984. 155 p.

437.   Hunt, Carroll Ferguson. *From the claws of the dragon.* Grand Rapids, MI : F. Asbury Press, 1988. 134 p.
On cover: *A story of deliverance from the Chinese Red Guards.*

438.   Johnson, Kay Ann. *Women, the family, and peasant revolution in China.* Chicago : University of Chicago Press, 1983. 282 p.
Focuses on Chinese Communist Party's policies from 1920s to 1979. Special chapter is devoted to the period of 1966 to 1969, and the criticism of Lin Biao and Confucius campaign in 1973 and 1974.

439. Kuriyama, Yoshihiro. *Political leadership and students in China (1966-1968) and France (1968)*. Thesis (Ph.D.). University of California, Berkeley, 1973. 273 leaves.

440. Lan Jiang. *A critical study of the May 7 Cadre School of the People's Republic of China during the Cultural Revolution, 1966-1976*. Thesis (M.S. Ed.). Northern Illinois University, 1989. 86 leaves.

441. Li Ting-sheng. *The CCP's persecution of Chinese intellectuals in 1949-69*. Taipei : Asian Peoples' Anti-Communist League, 1969. 67 p.
Examines the events before the Cultural Revolution, and discusses the re-education campaign during the Cultural Revolution.

442. *Model for revolutionary youth*. Peking : Foreign Languages Press, 1970. 50 p.
In memory of Jin Xunhua, a young student from Shanghai who sacrificed his life in Heilongjiang.

443. *New women in New China*. Peking : Foreign Languages Press, 1972. 78 p.

444. *On the re-education of intellectuals*. Peking : Foreign Languages Press, 1968. 11 p.
Translation of an article: Guan yu zhi shi fen zi zai jiao yu wen ti, which was originally written by the commentator of Renmin Ribao and Hongqi on September 12, 1968.

445. Raddock, David M. *Political behavior of adolescents in China : the Cultural Revolution in Kwang-chow*. Tuscon, AZ : Published for the Association for Asian Studies by the University of Arizona Press, 1977. 242 p.
Studies the attitudes of male adolescents toward participation in the Cultural Revolution in Guangzhou.

446. Rosen, Stanley. *Red Guard factionalism and the Cultural Revolution in Guangzhou (Canton)*. Boulder, CO : Westview Press, 1982. 320 p.
Studies the reasons behind the division of students into two large factions during the Cultural Revolution in Guangzhou. Analyzes internal divisions within the faction and subfactions showing the social bases for membership. Focuses on middle school students, but looks also at some university students.

447. Rosen, Stanley. *The role of sent down youth in the Chinese cultural revolution : the case of Guangzhou*. Berkeley : Institute of East Asian Studies & Center for Chinese Studies, University of California, 1981. 100 p.

448. Seybolt, Peter J., ed. *Rustication of urban youth in China : a social experiment*. White Plains, NY : M.E. Sharpe, 1977. 200 p.
Translation of: Re qing guan huai xia xiang zhi shi qing nian de cheng zhang, with several documents appended related to the transferring students to the countryside programs.

449. Sidel, Ruth. *Women and child care in China : firsthand report*. New York : Hill and Wang, 1972. 207 p.
Studies of family life in China and examines the effects of the dramatic political and social changes in the Cultural Revolution. It was largely based upon observations made in China in 1971.

450. Sidel, Ruth. *Women and child care in China : firsthand report*. Revised ed. New York : Penguin, 1982. 211 p.
This revised edition reproduces the original text except for the introduction and bibliography, which were rewritten and updated to 1981.

451. Singer, Martin. *Educated youth and the Cultural Revolution in China*. Ann Arbor, MI : University of Michigan, Center for Chinese Studies, 1971. 114 p.
Examines elements of Mao Zedong's vision of society, and the basic discontent among educated young people on the eve of the Cultural Revolution. Has a chronological review and reconstruction of the events of the Cultural Revolution as they affected young people.

452. *Take the road of integrating with the workers, peasants, and soldiers*. Peking : Foreign Languages Press, 1970. 94 p.

453. Thurston, Anne F. *Enemies of the People : the ordeal of the intellectuals in China's Great Cultural Revolution*. Cambridge, MA : Harvard University Press, 1988, c1987. 323 p.
Based largely on interviews conducted in China during the years 1981 and 1982, and the stories are told in substantial measure by victims of the Cultural Revolution.

454. Unger, Jonathan. *Education under Mao : class and competition in Canton schools, 1960-1980.* New York : Columbia University Press, 1982. 308 p.

455. Wang Hsueh-wen. *The awakening of Mainland youths from Mao's exploitation and persecution.* Taipei : Asian Peoples' Anti-Communist League, 1969. 92 p.

456. Webster, Norman. *Youth on march.* St. Paul, MN : EMC Corp., 1973. 48 p.
     Discusses the characteristics of China's youth and their schools, works, games, sports, and customs. This is one of Norman Webster's series *"Discovering today's China."*

457. Wolf, Margery. *Revolution postponed : women in contemporary China.* Stanford, CA : Stanford University Press, 1985. 285 p.

458. Yagoda, Maida Weissman. *Intra-party conflict and its effect on policies adopted towards the intellectuals prior to and during the Great Proletarian Cultural Revolution in the People's Republic of China.* Thesis (Ph.D.). New York University, 1977. 324 leaves.

459. Zang Xiaowei. *Children of the Cultural Revolution : class and caste in Mao's China. Thesis* (Ph.D. in Sociology). University of California, Berkeley, 1992. 224 leaves.

460. Zhang, Heather X. *Progress or retrogression for Chinese women? : the Cultural Revolution (1966-76) revisited.* Glasgow : Dept. of Government, University of Strathclyde, 1995. 35 p.

D. RELIGION

461. Chao, Jonathan. *A history of the church in China since 1949.* Grand Rapids, MI : Institute of Theological Studies, 1993. 12 sound cassettes + 1 study guide (52 p.).
     A series of twenty-four lectures on the history of the Christian church in China, presented by Jonathan Chao. Contents include: The Cultural Revolution and Christian suffering, 1966-1969 (Tape 5); The church under the Gang of Four, 1969-1976 (Tape 6).

462. MacInnis, Donald E. *Religion in China today : policy and practice.* Maryknoll, NY : Orbis Books, 1989. 458 p.
Provides some documents, articles, and press reports regarding the Chinese official policy on religion, and describes the actual religious situation in China using firsthand interviews, scholarly studies, speeches, reports, and journal articles.

463. Welch, Holms. *Buddhism under Mao.* Cambridge, MA : Harvard University Press, 1972. 666 p.

464. Xin Fang. *Buddhism before and after the Cultural Revolution.* Thesis (M.A.). Northern Illinois University, 1994. 117 leaves.

E. HEALTH CARE AND WELFARE

465. *Acupuncture anesthesia in the People's Republic of China : a trip report of the American Acupuncture Anesthesia Study Group, submitted to the Committee on Scholarly Communication with the People's Republic of China.* Washington, DC : National Academy of Sciences, 1976. 73 p.

466. Akhtar, Shahid. *Health care in the People's Republic of China : a bibliography with abstract.* Ottawa, Canada : International Development Research Centre, 1975. 182 p.
The majority of entries are published works, including books and journal articles.

467. *Barefoot doctor's manual : the American translation of the official Chinese paramedical manual.* New York : Running Press, 1977. 948 p.
A compilation of the techniques that Chinese barefoot doctors used in the countryside during the Cultural Revolution period, which includes certain acupuncture techniques and Chinese herbal medicine.

468. Dixon, John. *Chinese welfare system 1949-1979.* New York : Praeger, 1981. 437 p.
Consists of three parts: the welfare philosophy of the PRC; the welfare delivery system in the PRC; and the target groups, 1949-1979. Principal sources used are Chinese media translations, and secondary sources are trip and refugee reports and author's two trips to China.

469. Fu Weikang. *The story of Chinese acupuncture and moxibustion.* 1st ed. Peking : Foreign Languages Press, 1975. 40 p.

470. *Herbal pharmacology in the People's Republic of China : a trip report of the American Herbal Pharmacology Delegation : submitted to the Committee on Scholarly Communication with the People's Republic of China.* Washington, DC : National Academy of Sciences, 1975. 269 p.

471. Lampton, David, *The policies of medicine in China : the policy process, 1949-1977.* Boulder, CO : Westview Press, 1977. 301 p.
Exams and explains changes in Chinese health care policy during the period of 1949-1977.

472. Orleans, Leo A. *Health policies and services in China, 1974.* Washington, DC : U.S. Government Printing Office, 1974. 42 p.
Prepared for the Subcommittee of Health, the Committee on Labor and Public Welfare, United States Senate.

473. Sidel, Victor W. and Ruth Sidel. *Serve the people : observations on medicine in the People's Republic of China.* Boston : Beacon Press, 1974. 317 p.
Reprint of the edition published by Josiah Macy Foundation, New York, in series: Macy Foundation series on medicine and public health in China.
Topics include: development of health services; health care in the cities and countryside; medical education; health administration and research.

F. POPULATION

474. Coale, Ansley J. *Rapid population change in China, 1952-1982.* Washington, DC : National Academy Press, 1984. 103 p.

475. Congressional Research Service, Library of Congress. *China's birth rate, death rate, and population growth : another perspective : report.* Washington, DC : U.S. Government Printing Office, 1977. 31 p.
Prepared for the Committee on International Relations, U.S. House of Representatives.

476. Li Chengrui. *A study of China's population.* 1st ed. Beijing : Foreign Languages Press, 1992. 275 p.
Gives accounts of the past four population censuses and reliability of the respective statistics collected in 1953, 1964, 1982 and 1990. Points out

the grim population situation which China faces and possible solutions. Analyzes several forecasts on the prospects of Chinese population.

477. Orleans, Leo A. *Every fifth child : the population of China.* Stanford, CA : Stanford University Press, 1972. 191 p.
      Includes an appendix on the availability and nature of sources for research on China, and a comprehensive bibliography of sources relating to the study of the population in China.

478. State Statistical Bureau, P.R.C., comp. *China statistical yearbook, 1989.* New York : Praeger Publishers, 1990. 840 p.
      An English translation and revision of the official China Statistical Yearbook. It has about 1,000 statistical tables containing national and provincial data in social and economic fields for the year 1988, as well as major time series of national figures from 1949-1988.

479. Tien, H. Yuan. *China's population struggle : demographic decisions of the People's Republic, 1949-1969.* Columbus, OH : Ohio State University Press, 1973. 405 p.
      Examines China's demographic decisions. Includes measures affecting and affected by the existing population, examination of China's fertility-policy decisions, examination of social-policy measures that affect Chinese population trends in the longer run.

G. SCIENCE AND TECHNOLOGY

480. Berner, Boel. *China's science through visitors' eyes.* Lund : Research Policy Program, University of Lund, 1975. 58 leaves.
      Based on questionnaires returned by about two hundred Western scientists who visited China.

481. Chambers, David Wade. *Red and expert : a case study of Chinese science in the Cultural Revolution.* Revised ed. Victoria, Australia : Deakin University, 1984. 153 p.

482. *China : science walks on two legs.* New York : Avon Books, 1974. 316 p.
      A report of a visit to China in 1973 by a delegation of American scientists, organized as Science for the People. Tells how China has tried to make science and education more relevant to the need of the people.

483. Elzinga, Aant. *Red or expert : working notes on theory of science seen in the light of the Chinese revolutionary experience and Chinese science policy debate.* Goteborg : Institute for Theory of Science, University of Gothenburg, 1977-1978. 146 p. in 3 parts.
Contents: pt. 1. (lacks special title). pt. 2. Cultural Revolution. pt. 3. The debate, 1972-1976.

484. Kitching, Beverley M. *Science policy making in China since the Cultural Revolution.* Nathan, Qld., Australia : School of Modern Asian Studies, Griffith University, 1982. 75 p.

485. *Science and technology in the People's Republic of China.* Paris : Organisation for Economic Co-operation and Development ; Washington, DC : OECD Publication Center, 1977. 1 v.
Based on a seminar held in January 1976. Consists of twelve essays divided into five parts: economic development; science and science policy; manpower and education; technology and economic development; and the ideological context.

486. Wang, Yeu-Farn. *China's science and technology policy, 1949-1989.* Aldershot, Hants, England ; Brookfield, VT : Avebury, 1993. 173 p.

H. ECONOMICS

487. Andors, Stephen. *China's industrial revolution : politics, planning, and management, 1949 to the present.* 1st ed. New York : Pantheon Books, 1977. 344 p.
Last three chapters focus on the Cultural Revolution period. Includes studies on the politics, planning, and management in the Cultural Revolution, and China's industry since the Cultural Revolution.

488. Andors, Stephen, ed. *Workers and workplaces in revolutionary China.* White Plain, NY : M.E. Sharpe, 1977. 403 p.

489. Andors, Stephen. *Factory management in China : the politics of modernization in a revolutionary society, 1958-1969.* Thesis (Ph.D.). Columbia University, 1974. 567 leaves.

490. Axilrod, Eric. *The political economy of the Chinese revolution.* Hong Kong : Union Research Institute, 1972. 541 p.

491.   Bartke, Wolfgang. *Oil in the People's Republic of China : industry structure, production, exports.* Montreal : McGill-Queen's University Press, 1977. 125 p.
Translation of: Die Olwirtschaft der Volksrepublik China.

492.   Baum, Richard. *Revolution and reaction in rural China : the struggle between two roads during the Socialist Education Movement (1962-1966) and the Great Proletarian Cultural Revolution (1966-1968).* Thesis (Ph.D.). University of California, Berkeley, 1970. 383 leaves.

493.   Bettelheim, Charles. *Cultural revolution and industrial organization in China : changes in management and the division of labor.* New York : Monthly Review Press, 1974. 128 p.
Translation of: Revolution culturelle et organisation industrielle en Chine.
Examines the changes the Cultural Revolution had effected in the factories of China, including the changes of the organization of industrial work, its location, and its management patterns. The book relies largely on materials the author gathered during the trip to China in 1971.

494.   Brosseau, Maurice. *The cultural revolution in Chinese industry.* Thesis (Ph.D.). University of Chicago, 1982. 285 leaves.
Studies the effects of the Cultural Revolution on Chinese industry especially on machine-building and textile-manufacturing areas.

495.   Burns, John P. *Political participation in rural China.* Berkeley : University of California Press, 1988. 283 p.
Describes and analyzes the political action in rural China from 1962 to 1984.

496.   Chan, Leslie W. *The Taching Oilfield : Maoist model for economic development.* Canberra : Australian National University Press, 1974. 28 p.

497.   Cheng Chu-yuan. *The economy of Communist China, 1949-1969 : with a bibliography of selected materials on Chinese economic development.* Ann Arbor : University of Michigan, Center for Chinese Studies, 1971. 79 p.

498.   Cheng Shi. *A glance at China's economy.* Peking : Foreign Languages Press, 1974. 52 p.

499. *China : a reassessment of the economy, a compendium of papers submitted to the Joint Economic Committee of the Congress of the United States, July 10, 1975.* Washington, DC : U.S. Government Printing Office, 1975. 737 p.

500. Chu Li. *Inside a people's commune : report from Chiliying.* Peking : Foreign Languages Press, 1974. 212 p.
A report about the Qiliying People's Commune in Honan Province.

501. Crook, Frederick W. *Agricultural statistics of the People's Republic of China, 1949-86.* Washington, DC : U.S. Department of Agriculture, Economic Research Service, 1988. 158 p.

502. Domes, Jurgen. *Socialism in the Chinese countryside : rural societal policies in the People's Republic of China, 1949-1979.* London : C. Hurst & Co., 1980. 189 p.
Traces the development of rural societal policy in China since 1949 with special attention to the changes in the People's Commune system since 1958. The appendix offers English translation of three major Chinese Communist Party documents concerning the structures and functions of the people's commune.

503. Eckstein, Alexander. *China's economic revolution.* Cambridge, England : Cambridge University Press, c1977. 352 p.

504. Endicott, Stephen Lyon. *Red earth : revolution in a Sichuan village.* London : I. Tauris, 1988. 261 p.
A description of the changes that had taken place in the countryside since 1949. Based upon interviews as well as Chinese government documents, local records, and newspapers, it reveals through microcosm of village life the dynamics of China's revolutionary social, economic, and cultural transformation.

505. *Foreign trade of China, 1970-1979.* Tokyo : Institute of Development Economics, 1984. 334 p.
Translation of: Chugoku boeki jikeiretsuhyo, 1970-79-nen.
Contains chiefly statistical tables regarding commerce, exports, imports in China.

506. Garth, Bryant, ed. *China's changing role in the world economy.* New York : Praeger Publishers, 1975. 222 p.

Examines the complex economic and political issues concerning the development of China's economy and foreign trade.

507. Goodstadt, Leo. *China's search for plenty : the economics of Mao Tse-tung.* New York : Weatherhill, 1973. 266 p.
It was published in 1972 under the title: *Mao Tse Tung: the search for plenty.*

508. *Grasp revolution, promote production and win new victories on the industrial front.* Peking : Foreign Languages Press, 1969. 15 p.
Originally issued as a Renmin Ribao editorial.

509. Gurley, John G. *China's economy and the Maoist strategy.* New York : Monthly Review Press, 1976. 325 p.
Provides a detailed account of the progress of the Chinese economy from 1840 to the 1970s, especially from 1949 onward, and gives an examination of China's economic strategy and the way it has been translated into policies.

510. Howard, Roger. *"Grasp Revolution, Promote Production" : struggles over socialist construction in China, 1973-1976.* Thesis (Ph.D.). University of British Columbia, 1981. 358 leaves.

511. Howe, Christopher. *Wage patterns and wage policy in modern China, 1919-1972.* Cambridge, England : Cambridge University Press, 1973. 171 p.
Provides a statistical analysis of changes in the level and structure of Chinese wages from the 1920s to the early 1970s.

512. Hsiao, Gene T. *The foreign trade of China : policy, law, and practice.* Berkeley : University of California Press, 1977. 291 p.

513. Hua Guofeng. *Let the whole party mobilize for a vast effort to develop agriculture and build Tachai-type counties throughout the country : summing-up report at the National Conference on Learning from Tachai in Agriculture (October 15, 1975).* Peking : Foreign Languages Press, 1975. 72 p.
Translation of: Quan dang dong yuan, da ban nong ye, wei pu ji Dazhai xian er fen dou.

514.   Hung Yu-chiao. *The effect of cultural revolution on Chinese Communist's economy.* Taipei : Asian Peoples' Anti-Communist League, 1969. 62 p.

515.   Johnson, Elizabeth and Graham Johnson. *Walking on two legs : rural development in South China.* Ottawa, Canada : International Development Research Center, 1976. 72 p.
       Much of the information included is the result of a trip the authors took in 1973 to four communes in Guangdong Province.

516.   Kraus, Willy. *Economic development and social change in the People's Republic of China.* New York : Springer-Verlag, 1982. 432 p.
       Gives a survey of the concepts and goals, plans and measures, successes and failures of China in its efforts to promote economic and social development. It is based on the original German edition (1979): "Wirtschaftliche Entwicklung und sozialer Wandel in der Volksrepublik China."

517.   Kuo, Leslie T. C. (Leslie Tse-chiu). *Agriculture in the People's Republic of China : structural changes and technical transformation.* New York : Praeger Publishers, 1976. 288 p.

518.   Kwan, Yum K. (Yum-Keung) and Gregory C. Chow. *Estimating economic effects of the Great Leap Forward and the Cultural Revolution in China.* Hong Kong : Hong Kong University of Science and Technology, Department of Economics, 1995. 16 p.

519.   *Learning from Tachai in rural China.* Peking : Foreign Languages Press, 1975. 139 p.

520.   Lee, Peter N. S. *Industrial management and economic reform in China, 1949-1984.* Hong Kong : Oxford University Press, 1987. 355 p.
       Examines the changes in the policy output of industrial management at both the macro and the micro level in China after 1949. Studies the policy-making process in general, and focuses on the industrial management area in particular. Relies on documentary materials as well as visits to enterprise units and interviews in Beijing, Guangzhou and Hong Kong in the 1970s and 1980s.

521.   Li Min. *Red Flag Canal.* Peking : Foreign Languages Press, 1974. 61 p.
       A report on an irrigation canal system in Lin Xian, Henan Province.

522. Lockett, Martin. *Cultural revolution and industrial organization in a Chinese enterprise : the Beijing General Mill, 1966-1981.* Oxford : Templeton College, Oxford Centre for Management Studies, 1985. 47 p.

523. Lyons, Thomas P. *Economic integration and planning in Maoist China.* New York : Columbia University Press, 1987. 376 p.
It was originally presented as the author's Ph.D. thesis (Cornell University, 1983) under the title: *Economic integration and development in China, 1957-1979.*

524. Meisner, Mitchell R. *In Agriculture Learn from Dazhai theory and practice in Chinese rural development.* Thesis (Ph.D.). University of Chicago, 1977. 533 leaves.

525. *New China's first quarter-century.* Peking : Foreign Languages Press, 1975. 209 p.
Contents include topics: Shanghai's industry, Taching (Daqing) oil zone and Tachai (Dazhai), revolution in education, development in science and technology, barefoot doctor system.

526. Oksenberg, Michel, ed. *China's developmental experience.* New York : Academy of Political Science, 1973. 227 p.
Covers wide range of topics including agricultural development and technology, organization and application of science, environmental control, family life and care of the aging, the functions of schooling, bureaucracy, social changes, and social organization.

527. *People's Republic of China : an economic assessment, a compendium of papers submitted to the Joint Economic Committee of the congress of the United States.* Washington, DC : U.S. Government Printing Office, 1972. 382 p.

528. Perkins, Dwight Heald. *China's economic policy and performance during the Cultural Revolution and its aftermath.* Cambridge, MA : Harvard Institute for International Development, 1984. 76 p.

529. Perry, Elizabeth J., ed. *Putting class in its place : worker identities in East Asia.* Berkeley, CA : Institute of East Asian Studies, University of California, Berkeley, 1996. 250 p.
Contents include: "The Chinese Cultural Revolution in the factories : party-state structures and patterns of conflict / Andrew G. Walder."

530. Prybyla, Jan S. *The Chinese economy : problems and policies.*
      Columbia : University of South Carolina Press, 1978. 258 p.
      Contains studies on China's demography, agriculture, industry, banking,
      transportation, trade, health, education, and other areas.

531. Prybyla, Jan S. *Political economy of Communist China.* Scranton, PA :
      International Textbook Co., 1970. 605 p.
      Deals with the development of People's Republic of China's economy
      during the first two decades (1949-1969). Contents arranged in
      chronological order and divided into periods which roughly correspond
      to the shifts of the political power at the top and the corresponding
      changes in China's economic policy.

532. Qin Huailu;   William Hinton, ed. *Ninth heaven to ninth hell : the
      history of a noble Chinese experiment.* New York : Barricade Books,
      1995. 665 p.
      Constitutes a life story of Chen Yonggui, who was a farmer from the
      village of Dazai, became a national model, and in the early 1970s
      became the vice premier of the State Council.

533. *Red sun lights the road forward for Tachai.* Peking : Foreign Languages
      Press, 1969. 134 p.

534. Riskin, Carl. *China's political economy : the quest for development
      since 1949.* New York : Oxford University Press, 1987. 418 p.
      It is about the emergence of China as an industrializing nation in the
      second half of the twentieth century. The general organization of the
      book is chronological, in which the Chapter 8 focuses on the economic
      conflict and the Cultural Revolution, 1966-1976.

535. Robinson, Joan. *Economic management in China.* 2nd ed. London :
      Anglo-Chinese Educational Institute, 1975. 50 p.
      Mainly based upon a six-week trip to China made by the author, a
      Cambridge economist.

536. Shabad, Theodore. *China's changing map, national and regional
      development, 1949-1971.* New York : Praeger Publishers, 1972. 370 p.
      Traces the changes that have occurred on the map of China, both the
      political map of territorial-administrative organization and the economic
      map of resource development.

537. Smil, Vaclav. *China's energy : achievement, problems, prospects.* New York : Praeger, 1976. 246 p.

538. Sou, Jin-young. *The Tachai campaign and China's rural policy, 1964-1979.* Thesis (Ph.D.). University of Washington, 1980. 532 leaves.

539. Stavis, Benedict. *The politics of agricultural mechanization in China.* Ithaca : Cornell University Press, 1978. 288 p.
     A detailed analysis of how China has faced the political and social dimensions of one particular technology--agricultural mechanization.

540. *Struggle between the two roads in China's countryside.* Peking : Foreign Languages Press, 1968. 25 p.
     Translation of: Zhong guo nong cun liang tiao dao lu de dou zheng, an editorial of Renmin Ribao, Hongqi, and Jiefangjun Bao (November 23, 1967).

541. *Taching : red banner on China's industrial front.* Peking : Foreign Languages Press, 1972. 46 p.

542. Wheelwright, E. L. (Edward Lawrence) and Bruce McFarlane. *The Chinese road to socialism : economics of the Cultural Revolution.* New York : Monthly Review Press, 1970. 256 p.
     Studies on Chinese economic policies and the impact on the economy since 1957, especially on the Cultural Revolution period from 1966 to 1968. The first section outlines economic developments up to 1966. The second section examines the significance of the Cultural Revolution.

543. Whitson, William W., ed. *Doing business with China : American trade opportunities in the 1970s.* New York : Praeger, 1974. 593 p.
     Essays on several aspects of trading with China, from how to approach China's foreign trade corporations to the proper social and negotiating etiquette.

544. Wong, John H. G. (John Heet-Ghin). *Agricultural development and peasant behavior in China during the cultural revolution.* Thesis (Ph.D.). Massachusetts Institute of Technology, 1992. 192 leaves.

545. Xin Huawen. *Tachai, standard bearer in China's agriculture.* Peking : Foreign Languages Press, 1972. 29 p.

546. Yang, Dali L. *Calamity and reform in China : state, rural society, and institutional change since the great leap famine*. Stanford, CA : Stanford University Press, 1996. 351 p.
Studies the political economy of the Great Leap Forward and the famine aftermath, the structural incentives for rural reform, and the political struggle over reform. It has one chapter devoted to the Cultural Revolution and its impact on the Chinese rural society.

547. Zweig, David. *Agrarian radicalism in China*. Cambridge, MA : Harvard University Press, 1989. 269 p.
Explains the variations in local support and opposition for the radical line in Chinese agriculture during the period of 1968-1978.

I. LAW AND LEGISLATION

548. *Analysis of the Draft of the revised constitution of the Chinese Communist regime*. Taipei : World Anti-Communist League, 1971. 137 p.
A comparative analysis of the new and old P.R.C. constitution.

549. Bilancia, Philip R. *Dictionary of Chinese law and government, Chinese-English*. Stanford, CA : Stanford University Press, 1981. 822 p.

550. Chiu, Hungdah. *Agreements of the People's Republic of China : a calendar of events, 1966-1980*. New York : Praeger, 1981. 331 p.
References are presented in chronological sequence with separate sections for bilateral and multilateral agreements.

551. Chiu, Hungdah. *The People's Republic of China and the law of treaties*. Cambridge, MA : Harvard University Press, 1972. 178 p.

552. Cohen, Jerome Alan and Hungdah Chiu, comps. *People's China and international law : a documentary study*. Princeton, NJ : Princeton University Press, 1974. 2 v. (1,790 p.).
A compilation of treaties, cables, government statements, and other documents. Includes an English-Chinese glossary of over 500 terms and a comprehensive bibliography.

553. *Constitution of the People's Republic of China*. 1st ed. Peking : Foreign Languages Press, 1975. 61 p.

This constitution was adopted by the National People's Congress on January 17, 1975.

554. Heinzig, Dieter. *Disputed islands in the South China Sea : Paracels, Spratlys, Pratas, Macclesfield Bank*. Wiesbaden : Harrassowitz, 1976. 46, 12 p.

555. Ho, Paul, comp. *The People's Republic of China and international law : a selective bibliography of Chinese sources*. Washington, DC : Library of Congress, 1972. 45 p.

556. Hsiao, Gene T. *Communist China's foreign trade contracts and means of settling disputes*. Berkeley, CA : Center for Chinese Studies, University of California, Berkeley, 1969. 503-529 p.
It is the China Series Reprint, no. C-11. Reprinted from Vanderbilt Law Review, vol. 22, no. 3 (April 1969).

557. Hsiao, Gene T. *The foreign trade of China : policy, law, and practice*. Berkeley, CA : University of California Press, 1977. 291 p.

558. Johnston, Douglas M. *Agreements of the People's Republic of China, 1949-1967 : a calendar*. Cambridge, MA : Harvard University Press, 1968. 286 p.

559. Leng, Shao Chuan and Hungdah Chiu, comps. *Law in Chinese foreign policy : Communist China and selected problems of international law*. New York : Oceana, 1972. 387 p.
Examines the international legal positions taken by China with regard to the UN, the outer space, and other issues, and also the status of Taiwan issue.

560. Li, Victor H., ed. *Law and politics in China's foreign trade*. Seattle : University of Washington Press, 1977. 467 p.
Updated papers of a conference held at the Contemporary China Institute, School of Oriental and African Studies, London in 1971.

561. Rhode, Grant F. and Reid E. Whitlock. *Treaties of the People's Republic of China, 1949-1978 : an annotated compilation*. Boulder, CO : Westview Press, 1980. 207 p.
Treaties listed in five groups: friendship, boundaries, commerce, consular, and dual nationality.

J. FOREIGN POLICIES AND FOREIGN RELATIONS

562. Abidi, Aqil Hyder Hasan. *China, Iran, and the Persian Gulf.* Atlantic Highlands, NJ : Humanities Press, 1982. 325 p.
Most of the work deals with relations with the Shah before the Iranian Revolution.

563. Allen, Thomas Harrell. *An examination of the communicative interaction between the United States and the People's Republic of China from January 1969 to February 1972.* Thesis (Ph.D.). Ohio State University, 1973. 126 leaves.

564. Ambroz, Oton. *Realignment of world power : the Russo-Chinese schism under the impact of Mao Tse-tung's last revolution.* New York : R. Speller, 1972. 2 v.

565. An, Tai Sung. *The Sino-Soviet territorial dispute.* Philadelphia : Westminster Press, 1973. 254 p.
Chapter 3 focuses on the 1969 Sino-Soviet battle over the Island Zhenbao (Damansky) in the Ussuri River.

566. Armstrong, J. D. (James David) *Revolutionary diplomacy : Chinese foreign policy and the united front doctrine.* Berkeley : University of California Press, 1977. 251 p.
Studies what the influence of Mao Zedong's united front doctrine has been on China's foreign policy, and in what ways China's participation in the international system has caused it to revise its conception of a united front in world politics.

567. Barnds, William J., ed. *China and America : the search for a new relationship.* New York : New York University Press, 1977. 254 p.

568. Barnett, A. Doak. *A new U.S. policy toward China.* Washington, DC : Brookings Institution, 1971. 132 p.
Examines the Sino-American relations, and discusses them in three parts: historical background and current setting; question relating to Taiwan, UN membership problem, nuclear issue; and a concluding section.

569. Barnouin, Barbara and Yu Changgen. *Chinese foreign policy during the Cultural Revolution.* London ; New York : Kegan Paul International ; New York : Distributed by Columbia University Press, 1997. 252 p.

Examines the effect the Cultural Revolution had on the Chinese Ministry of Foreign Affairs. Focuses on the decision-making process in Chinese foreign policy. Studies the conflict between traditionalists and the defenders of new revolutionary concepts, and the impact this had on the implementation of foreign policy.

570. Bawden, C. R. (Charles R.). *Some remarks on the relationship between China and Mongolia.* London : The China Society, 1974. 17 p.

571. Behbehani, Hashim S. H. *China's foreign policy in the Arab world, 1955-75 : three case studies.* London : Kegan Paul International, 1981. 426 p.
Describes China's foreign policy by using three case studies: Chinese policy toward the several groups that comprised the Palestine resistance movement; Chinese policy toward the evolving organizations of the national liberation movement in Oman; and Chinese policy to gain diplomatic recognition from Kuwait. It divides China's policy into three chronological phrases: 1955-1966, 1966-1970, and 1970-1975.

572. Biberaj, Elez. *Albania and China : a study of an unequal alliance.* Boulder, CO : Westview Press, 1986. 183 p.
Analyzes the relationship between Albania's political allegiance to China, and China's economic, military, and political assistance to Albania, and demonstrates how Tirana extracted considerable concessions from Beijing. This study recounts the emergence of political, ideological, and economic differences between these two countries, and examines the national and international developments that produced the estrangement.

573. Boardman, Robert. *Britain and the People's Republic of China, 1949-74.* New York : Barnes & Noble Books, 1976. 210 p.
A study of British attitudes and policies towards China by looking in depth at several aspects and periods. Chapter 8 is a study of the period of 1967-1974, from the low point in relations brought about by the Cultural Revolution to the exchange ambassadors in 1972.

574. Borisov, Oleg Borisovich and B. T. Koloskov. *Soviet-Chinese relations, 1945-1970.* Bloomington : Indiana University, 1975. 364 p.
It is the official Soviet record of conflict with China as seen from the perspective of Moscow in 1971, written by two high-ranking specialists in Chinese affairs.

575. Buss, Claude Albert. *China : the People's Republic of China and Richard Nixon.* San Francisco : Freeman & Co., 1972. 118 p.

576. Calabrese, John. *China's changing relations with the Middle East.* London ; New York : Pinter, 1991. 183 p.
A review of China's involvement in the Middle East which evolved during the four decades following the establishment of the People's Republic of China in 1949.

577. Camilleri, Joseph A. *Chinese foreign policy : the Maoist era and its aftermath.* Seattle : University of Washington Press, 1981. 311 p.
Examines three phases of Chinese foreign policy: a revolutionary period (1949-68), a transitional period (1969-1976), and a post-revolutionary period (1977 onward).

578. Chai, Winberg, ed. *Foreign relations of the People's Republic of China.* New York : Putnam, 1972. 420 p.
Consists of sixty-six documents, treaties, correspondence, and policy statements.

579. *Chairman Mao's theory of the differentiation of the three world's is a major contribution to Marx-Leninism.* 1st ed. Peking : Foreign Languages Press, 1977. 79 p.

580. Chavan, R. S. *Chinese foreign policy : the Chou En-lai era.* 1st ed. New Delhi : Sterling, 1979. 261 p.

581. Chen, King C., ed. *China and the three worlds : a foreign policy reader.* White Plains, NY : M.E. Sharpe, 1979. 383 p.

582. *China : US policy since 1945.* Washington, DC : U.S. Government Printing Office for the Congressional Quarterly, 1980. 387 p.
A revision and updating of a 1968 Congressional Quarterly publication. Contains a chronology of events between 1945 and 1980, biographical sketches of Chinese leaders, text of documents, and a number of maps, charts and other information.

583. *China's great revolution and the Soviet Union's great tragedy.* Peking : Foreign Languages Press, 1967. 14 p.
An article written by the Renmin Ribao observer, June 4, 1967.

584. *Chinese-Korean friendship--deep-rooted and flourishing : the party and government delegation of the Democratic People's Republic of Korea visits China.* Peking : Foreign Languages Press, 1975. 67 p.

585. *Chinese people firmly support the Arab people's struggle against aggression.* Peking : Foreign Languages Press, 1967. 52 p.

586. Choudhury, G. W. (Golam Wahed). *China in world affairs : the foreign policy of the PRC since 1970.* Boulder, CO : Westview Press, 1982. 310 p.
      A review of China's foreign policy during the period of 1970-1981. Examines China's global policy, diplomatic options, and the relations with U.S. and Soviet Union. Includes topics on China's quest for security, the breakthrough in China-U.S. relations, China's role in the UN since 1971, how China has championed Third World countries, and China's post-Mao foreign policy.

587. Chung, Chin-wi. *Pyongyang between Peking and Moscow : North Korea's involvement in the Sino-Soviet dispute, 1958-1975.* University, AL : University of Alabama Press, 1978. 230 p.
      An examination of North Korea's attitude in the Sino-Soviet dispute and of why and how the North Korean reacted to the specific issues and events in Sino-Soviet relations from 1958 through 1975. Author's name on the title page: Chin O. Chung.

588. Cohen, Jerome Alan et al. *Taiwan and American policy : the dilemma in U.S.-China relations.* New York : Praeger Publishers, 1971. 191 p.
      It is the proceedings of a conference held on March 5th and 6th, 1971, in Washington DC.

589. *Comment on the Soviet-West German treaty.* Peking : Foreign Languages Press, 1970. 38 p.
      An article written by the Renmin Ribao commentator, Sept. 13, 1970.

590. Copper, John Franklin. *China's foreign aid : an instrument of Peking's foreign policy.* Lexington, MA : Lexington Books, 1976. 197 p.
      A survey of China's foreign aid programs in North Vietnam, North Korea, and other countries particularly in Asia and Africa.

591. Deng Xiaoping. *Speech by chairman of the delegation of the People's Republic of China, Teng Hsiao-ping, at the special session of the UN*

General Assembly, April 10, 1974. Peking : Foreign Languages Press, 1974. 22 p.

592.   Dickinson, William B., ed.   *China and U.S. foreign policy.* 2nd ed. Washington, DC : Congressional Quarterly Inc., 1973. 103 p.

593.   Dittmer, Lowell.   *Sino-Soviet normalization and its international implications, 1945-1990.* Seattle : University of Washington Press, 1992. 373 p.

594.   *Down with the new tsars! : Soviet revisionists' anti-China atrocities on Heilung and Wusuli Rivers.* Peking : Foreign Languages Press, 1969. 1 v.

595.   Ebinger, Putnam Mundy.   *The politics of potential : the relations of the People's Republic of China and the European Community and its member-states France and Great Britain, 1969-1979.* Thesis (Ph.D.). Fletcher School of Law and Diplomacy, Tufts University, 1988. 475 leaves.

596.   Fitzgerald, C. P. (Charles Patrick).   *China and South-east Asia since 1945.* London : Studies in Contemporary China, 1973. 110 p.
Includes country-by-country survey dealing with Vietnam, Cambodia, Laos, Indonesia, Burma, Thailand, Philippines, Malaysia, and Singapore, followed by a brief discussion about China's relations with the overseas Chinese and ethnic Chinese communities.

597.   Garver, John W.   *China's decision for rapprochement with the United States, 1968-1971.* Boulder, CO : Westview Press, 1982. 174 p.
A detailed account of the events leading to China's move toward rapprochement with the United States.

598.   Garver, John W.   *Foreign relations of the People's Republic of China.* Englewood Cliffs, NJ : Prentice-Hall, 1993. 340 p.
Covers major aspects of modern China's foreign relations--from China's relations with ethnic Chinese communities in Southeast Asia, and the wars China has fought, to its efforts to acquire foreign technology, its role in the UN, and its relations with foreign revolutionary movements.

599.   Ghoble, T. R. (Trimbak Ramrao).   *China's foreign policy : opening to the West.* New Delhi : Deep & Deep Publications, 1989. 252 p.

600.   Gittings, John. *Survey of the Sino-Soviet dispute : a commentary and extracts from the recent polemics 1963-1967.* London : Oxford University Press, 1968. 410 p.
Extracts, refines, and interprets passages from the polemics, and presents them in a form from which easy reference can be made. Includes documents published by both sides from 1963 onwards.

601.   Gottlieb, Thomas M. *Chinese foreign policy factionalism and the origins of the strategic triangle : a report prepared for Director of Net Assessment, Office of the Secretary of Defense.* Santa Monica, CA : Rand, 1977. 145 p.

602.   Gurtov, Melvin. *The foreign ministry and foreign affairs in China's "cultural revolution."* Santa Monica, CA : Rand, 1969. 83 leaves.

603.   Hefron, Peter Oslin. *Ideology and Chinese foreign policy during the Eighth Central Committee, 1956-1969.* Thesis (Ph.D.). Fletcher School of Law and Diplomacy, Tufts University, 1976. 614 leaves.

604.   Hinton, Harold C. *The bear and the gate : Chinese policy making under Soviet pressure.* Washington, DC : American Enterprise Institute for Public Policy Research, 1971. 112 p.

605.   Hinton, Harold C. *China's turbulent quest : an analysis of China's foreign relations since 1949.* Bloomington, IN : Indiana University Press, 1972. 352 p.
It begins with an examination of Maoism, Sino-Soviet relations, the confrontations in Korea and Vietnam, and the Cultural Revolution. The second section is concerned with Chinese foreign policy and military strategy. The third section summarizes China's complex role in world affairs.

606.   Holbo, Paul Sothe. *United States policies toward China : from the unequal treaties to the cultural revolution.* New York : Macmillan, 1969. 107 p.

607.   Holdridge, John H. *Crossing the divide : an insider's account of normalization of U.S.-China relations.* Lanham, MD : Rowman & Littlefield, 1997. 307 p.
Provides the insider's account of U.S.-China relations in the 1970s and 1980s, from the secret flight to Beijing in 1970 and Nixon's China trip in 1972, to the Carter and Reagan years.

608.   Horvath, Janos. *Chinese technology transfer to the Third World : a grants economy analysis.* New York : Praeger, 1976. 101 p.

609.   House Committee on Foreign Affairs, U.S. Congress. *New China policy : its impact on the United States and Asia.* Washington, DC : U.S. Government Printing Office, 1972. 310 p.
       Hearings of Ninety-second U.S. Congress, Second Session, May 2, 3, 4, 16 and 17, 1972.

610.   Hsiao, Shi-ching. *Chinese-Philippine diplomatic relations, 1946-1975.* Quezon City, Philippines : Bookman Print House, 1975. 317 p.

611.   Hussain, Hamid. *China's third world policy at United Nations, 1971-1981.* Thesis (Ph.D.). New Delhi : Jawaharial Nehru University, 1983. 1 v.

612.   Hutchison, Alan. *China's African revolution.* Boulder, CO : Westview Press, 1976. 313 p.

613.   *Irresistible historical trend.* Peking : Foreign Languages Press, 1971. 47 p.
       Contents include: Statement of the Government of the People's Republic of China; Telegrams from Ji Pengfei; Text of the UN resolution drafted by Albania and twenty-one other countries; UN General Assembly voting results; Speech by Qiao Guanhua at UN; Renmin Ribao editorial.

614.   Isenberg, Irwin, ed. *China : new force in world affairs.* New York : H.W. Wilson, 1972. 219 p.
       A compilation of articles presenting various points of view on the life and government policy in China.

615.   Jain, Rajendra Kumar. *China and Japan, 1949-1976.* Atlantic Highlands, NJ : Humanities Press, 1977. 336 p.

616.   Jain, Rajendra Kumar. *China and Japan, 1949-1980.* Thoroughly rev. and expanded 2nd ed. Oxford : M. Robertson, 1981. 339 p.

617.   Jain, Rajendra Kumar, ed. *China and Malaysia, 1949-1983.* New Delhi : Radiant, 1984. 364 p.

618.   Jain, Rajendra Kumar, ed. *China and Thailand, 1949-1983 : documents.* New Delhi : Radiant, 1984. 415 p.

619. Jain, Rajendra Kumar. *China, Pakistan and Bangladesh*. New Delhi : Radiant, 1974. 270 p.
Examines the Sino-Indo-Pakistan relations from 1952 to the war of 1971 in Bangladesh.

620. Jansen, Maurius B. *Japan and China : from war to peace 1894-1972*. Chicago : Rand McNally College Publishing Co., 1975. 547 p.
Contains twelve essays which move chronologically from the Sino-Japanese war of 1894-95 to the normalization of relations in 1972.

621. Jensen, Daniel Delano. *Nixon's trip to China, 1972 : three views*. Thesis (Doctoral). Illinois State University, 1982. 177 leaves.

622. Kau, Michael Y. M. and Christopher J. Szymanski. *The Chinese Foreign Ministry elite and the Cultural Revolution*. Edwardsville : Southern Illinois University at Edwardsville, 1973. 21 p.

623. Keith, Ronald C. *The diplomacy of Zhou Enlai*. New York : St. Martin's Press, 1989. 268 p.
Focuses on a chronological study of the schematic framework that Zhou Enlai developed his work style, strategies, and policies so as to achieve a realistic and successful diplomacy. Contents include "Chapter 6: The 'Revolutionary diplomatic line' in the Cultural Revolution" and "Chapter 7: Strategy and 'Realism' in Sino-American normalization."

624. Kim, Samuel S. *China, the United Nations, and world order*. Princeton, NJ : Princeton University Press, 1979. 581 p.
An analysis of China's participation in the United Nations, focusing on the years 1971-1977.

625. Kim, Young Mun. *Chinese foreign policy toward the third worlds in the 1970's, the theory and practice of the three worlds*. Thesis (Ph.D.). University of California, Riverside, 1979. 379 leaves.

626. Kissinger, Henry. *The White House years*. London : Weidenfeld, 1979. 1,521 p.
Memoirs cover Kissinger's years as President Nixon's National Security Adviser in the first Nixon Administration (1969-1972). Describes the initial "Ping-Pong diplomacy" in Chapter 18, secret journey to Beijing in Chapter 19, and Nixon's visit to China (1972) in Chapter 24.

627. Kubek, Anthony. *The Red China papers : what Americans deserve to know about U.S.-Chinese relations.* New Rochelle, NY : Arlington House Publishers, 1975. 255 p.
Provides the central facts of the Chinese-American relationship over its extended history, and highlights the several crises in three decades, from 1945 to 1975.

628. Larkin, Bruce D. *China and Africa, 1949-1970 : the foreign policy of the People's Republic of China.* Berkeley, CA : University of California Press, 1971. 268 p.
A study of Chinese political and economic activities in African countries.

629. Lawson, Eugene K. *Sino-Vietnamese conflict.* New York : Praeger Publishers, 1984. 324 p.
Documents in detail of the relationships between China and Vietnam especially during the 1964-1975 period.

630. Lim, Heng-cheah. *The foreign policy of the Chinese People's Republic toward Pakistan, 1958-1969.* Thesis (Ph.D.). Queen's University at Kingston, 1972. 428 leaves.

631. Lovelace, Daniel Dudley. *China and "people's war" in Thailand, 1964-1969.* Berkeley : Center for Chinese Studies, University of California, 1973. 101 p.

632. Low, Alfred D. *The Sino-Soviet dispute.* Madison, NJ : Fairleigh Dickinson University Press, 1978. 364 p.
A combination of the chronological and topical approach to trace and analyze Soviet and Chinese policies toward each other during the period of 1956-1973. Contents include "Chapter 8: From the Cultural Revolution to military conflict, 1965-1969" and "Chapter 9: Peking's reversal of isolationism. The Soviet response, 1969 to the present (1973)."

633. Mozingo, David P. *Chinese policy toward Indonesia 1949-1967.* Ithaca, NY : Cornell University Press, 1976. 303 p.
An analysis and explanation of the Sino-Indonesian relationship during two decades. Studies the major successes and failures of Chinese diplomacy in Indonesia.

634. Naik, J. A. *India, Russia, China and Bangladesh*. New Delhi : Chand, 1972. 163 p.
A critical study of the policies of Beijing and Moscow during the 1971 civil war in Pakistan, which resulted in the creation of Bangladesh.

635. Nixon, Richard. *The memoirs of Richard Nixon*. London : Sidgwick and Jackson, 1978. 1,120 p.
The memoirs include a description of his historic visit to China in 1972, and record conversations with Mao Zedong and Zhou Enlai.

636. *Normalizing relations with the People's Republic of China : problems, analysis and documents*. Baltimore : University of Maryland Law School, 1978. 207 p.
Edited by Hungdah Chiu.

637. Ogunsanwo, Alaba. *China's policy in Africa, 1958-71*. New York : Cambridge University Press, 1974. 310 p.

638. *Premier Chou En-lai pays friendship visit to Korea*. Peking : China Reconstructs, 1970. 25 p.

639. *Premier Chou En-lai visits the Democratic People's Republic of Korea*. Peking : Foreign Languages Press, 1970. 96 p.

640. Qiao Guanhua. *Speech*. Peking : Foreign Languages Press, 1975. 34 p.
Speech at the plenary meeting of the 30th Session of the UN General Assembly in 1975.

641. Qiao Guanhua. *Speech by Chiao Kuan-hua, chairman of the delegation of the People's Republic of China, at the plenary meeting of the 28th Session of the UN General Assembly, October 2, 1973*. Peking : Foreign Languages Press, 1973. 26 p.

642. Qiao Guanhua. *Speech by Chiao Kuan-hua, chairman of the delegation of the People's Republic of China, at the plenary meeting of the 29th Session of the UN General Assembly (October 2, 1974)*. Peking : Foreign Languages Press, 1974. 26 p.

643. *Relations between the Federal Republic of Germany and the People's Republic of China, Oct. 1972-Dec. 1977, as seen by Hsinhua News Agency : a documentation*. Hamburg : Institute of Asian Affairs, 1978. 597 p.

Compiled by Wolfgang Brake.

644. Ro. Kwang H. (Kwang Hai) and Thomas D. Wu. *China : rise of*
      communism, and foreign relations since 1949. Washington, DC :
      University Press of America, 1977. 239 p.
      Describes and examines the modernization process of China's political
      and foreign affairs. Provides information of the origin and development
      of Chinese communism, and analyzes the foreign relations since 1949.

645. Robinson, Thomas W. *The Sino-Soviet dispute : background, develop-*
      ment, and the March 1969 clashes. Santa Monica, CA : Rand, 1970. 74
      p.

646. Russell, Maud. *The Sino-Soviet Ussuri River border clash : the*
      historical background and current implications. New York : Maud
      Russell, 1969? 24 p.

647. Salisbury, Harrison Evans. *War between Russia and China.* New York :
      Norton & Co., 1969. 224 p.
      The book was written out of concern over the tension between the Soviet
      Union and China, and the proliferation of signs that the two countries
      were headed toward a collision course and war.

648. Shambaugh, David L. *China and Europe, 1949-1995.* London :
      Contemporary China Institute, School of Oriental and African Studies,
      University of London, 1996. 74 p.

649. Shao Kuo-kang. *Zhou Enlai and the foundations of Chinese foreign*
      policy. New York : St. Martin's Press, 1996. 370 p.
      A comprehensive survey of China's foreign relations from 1949 to 1976
      focusing on the significant role Zhou Enlai played. It studies Chinese
      foreign relations with the United States, the Soviet Union, and Third
      World countries, as well as Zhou Enlai's negotiating skills.

650. Pearson, Roger, ed. *Sino-Soviet intervention in Africa.* Washington,
      DC : Council on American Affairs, 1977. 103 p.

651. *Sino-U.S. joint communiqué (February 28, 1972).* Peking : Foreign Lan-
      guages Press, 1972. 7 p.

652. Smith, Jack A. *Unite the many, defeat the few : China's revolutionary*
      line in foreign affairs. New York : Guardian, 1973. 38 p.

653.   Smyser, William Richard. *North Vietnam and the Sino-Soviet conflict, 1956-1969.* Thesis. George Washington University, 1977. 364 leaves.

654.   Solomon, Richard H. *Chinese political negotiating behavior, 1967-1984.* Santa Monica, CA : Rand, 1985. 188 p.
A study of Chinese officials' political negotiating behavior with the U.S. during the 'normalization' phase of relations between the two countries. Provides guidance for senior American officials prior to their first negotiating encounters with Chinese counterparts and to establish control over the documentary record of U.S.-China political exchanges between 1967 and 1984.

655.   *Speeches welcoming the delegation of the People's Republic of China by the UN General Assembly President and representatives of various countries, at the plenary meeting of the 26th session of the UN General Assembly (November 15, 1971).* Peking : Foreign Languages Press, 1971. 158 p.

656.   Sutter, Robert G. *Chinese foreign policy after the cultural revolution, 1966-1977.* Boulder, CO : Westview Press, 1978. 176 p.

657.   Szymanski, Christopher J. *Bureaucratic development in the People's Republic of China : a case study of the foreign affairs system, 1949-1973.* Thesis (Ph.D.). Brown University, 1975. 194 leaves.

658.   Taylor, Jay. *China and Southeast Asia : Peking's relations with revolutionary movements.* New York : Praeger Publishers, 1974. 376 p.
A critical study and analysis of China's internal debate and its effect on foreign policy between 1965 and 1972, including chapters on Vietnam, Indonesia, Burma, Thailand, Malaysia, Singapore, and other countries and areas.

659.   Thornton, Richard C. *The bear and the dragon : Sino-Soviet relations and the political evolution of the Chinese People's Republic, 1949-1971.* New York : American-Asian Educational Exchange, 1972. 72 p.

660.   Tretiak, Daniel. *The Chinese cultural revolution & foreign policy : the process of conflict & current policy.* Waltham, MA : Westinghouse Electric Corp., Advanced Studies Group, 1970. 36 leaves.

661.   Tsui Tien-hua. *The Sino-Soviet border dispute in the 1970s.* Oakville, Ontario : Mosai Press, 1984. 151 p.

An analysis of the historical evolution of the border, the frontier confrontation in the 1970s, the border negotiation after 1969, and the different public opinions from Chinese and Soviet media regarding each country's position.

662. Van Ness, Peter. *Revolution and Chinese foreign policy : Peking's support for wars of national liberation.* Berkeley : University of California Press, 1970. 266 p.
A study of Chinese foreign policy and how support for foreign revolution fits into that policy. Contents include "Part 3: The Great Proletarian Cultural Revolution and Chinese foreign policy."

663. Wang Miao. *Impact of the Great Proletarian Cultural Revolution on Communist China's foreign policy.* Thesis. University of Oklahoma, 1978. 231 leaves.

664. Warren, Susan. *China's voice in the United Nations.* New York : World Winds Press, 1974. 176 p.
Contains speeches and statements made by the Chinese delegation at the UN's 28th session and 6th special session in 1973 and 1974.

665. Waterman, Lillian Harris. *People's Republic of China and the Palestine question, 1950-September 9, 1976.* Thesis (Ph.D.). Georgetown University, 1977. 327 leaves.

666. Wedeman, Andrew Hall. *The east wind subsides : Chinese foreign policy and the origins of the Cultural Revolution.* Washington, DC : Washington Institute Press, c1987. 317 p.

667. Whiting, Allen Suess. *Chinese domestic politics and foreign policy in the 1970s.* Ann Arbor, MI : Center for Chinese Studies, University of Michigan, 1977. 85 p.

668. *Why the imperialist-revisionist chorus frenziedly attacks the Communist Party of China and the Chinese great proletarian cultural revolution.* Tirana : Naim Frasheri, 1966. 38 p.
Reproduced from the "Zeri I populit" daily, dated Dec. 29, 1966.

669. Wich, Richard. *Sino-Soviet crisis politics : a study of political change and communication.* Cambridge, MA : Council on East Asian Studies, 1980. 313 p.

It selects the 1968-1971 period to study the Sino-Soviet crisis and the political changes. Focuses on the effects of the August 1968 Soviet invasion of Czechoslovakia, the Ussuri clashes of March 1969, and the Vietnam war.

670. Wishnick, Elizabeth Anne. *Ideology and Soviet policy towards China, 1969-89*. Thesis (Ph.D.). Columbia University, 1992. 417 leaves.

671. Wu Yuan-li. *The strategic ridge : Peking's relations with Thailand, Malaysia, Singapore and Indonesia*. Stanford, CA : Hoover Institution, 1975. 97 p.

672. Yu, George T. *China and Tanzania : study in cooperative interaction*. Berkeley : Center for Chinese Studies, University of California, 1970. 100 p.
A study of China's foreign policy reorientation. Consists of an investigation of its policy and behavior toward Tanzania and concerns mainly with the form of the relationship as well as with the behavior within the relationship. Includes a case study of "the Tanzania-Zambia Railway."
Documents: p. 80-100.

673. Yu, George T. *China's African policy : a study of Tanzania*. New York : Praeger Publishers, 1975. 200 p.
Examines one dimension of China's foreign-policy reorientation in the mid-1970s, and consists of an investigation of its policy and behavior toward Tanzania.

674. Zagoria, Donald S. *Vietnam triangle : Moscow, Peking, Hanoi*. New York : Pegasus, 1967. 286 p.

K. SOCIAL LIFE

675. Ascher, Isaac. *China's social policy*. 2nd ed. London : Anglo-Chinese Educational Institute, 1976. 79 p.

676. Chan, Anita, Richard Madsen, and Jonathan Unger. *Chen Village : the recent history of a peasant community in Mao's China*. Berkeley : University of California Press, 1984. 293 p.
Examines the changes that have occurred in the lives of the people of a South China farming village in the 1960s and 1970s. Illustrates the

impact of a series of tumultuous political campaigns over the two decades in one such community.

677. Chan, Anita, Richard Madsen, and Jonathan Unger. *Chen Village under Mao and Deng : the recent history of a peasant community in Mao's China.* 2nd ed. Berkeley : University of California Press, 1992. 345 p.
Expanded and updated edition of: *Chen Village.* 1984.

678. Chance, Norman Allee. *China's urban village : life in a Beijing commune.* New York : Holt, 1984. 165 p.
A report of a fieldwork in a Beijing commune between 1972 and 1978. Provides detailed descriptions of the customs surrounding childbirth through marriage, as well as the family life in the commune.

679. Chen, Jack. *A year in Upper Felicity : life in a Chinese village during the Cultural Revolution.* New York : Macmillan, 1973. 383 p.
Presents a personal account of daily life in a rural village, and describes the relationship between the cadres and villagers. The author as an associate editor in the Peking Review was transformed to the countryside in 1968.

680. Fan, K. T. *The making of the new human being in the People's Republic of China.* New York : Maud Russell, 1974. 48 p.

681. Frolic, B. Michael. *Mao's people : sixteen portraits of life in revolutionary China.* Cambridge, MA : Harvard University Press, 1980. 278 p.
A collection of stories selected from interviews with people moved from various places in China and lived in Hong Kong. The coverage is broad, from the late 1960s through the mid-1970s and from the South China to the North China including urban life, rural life, and in between.

682. Hinton, William. *'Fanshen' re-examined in the light of the cultural revolution.* Boston : New England Free Press, 1969. 1 v.

683. Hinton, William. *Shenfan : the continuing revolution in a Chinese village.* London : Secker and Warburg, 1983. 789 p.
This work is author's account of his life in a Chinese village and his return to that village in 1971. It supplies with an amount of data on the village's economic, social, and political changes from 1948 to 1971.

684. Kraus, Richard Curt. *Class conflict in Chinese socialism*. New York : Columbia University Press, 1981. 243 p.
Examines how the politics, ideology, and class struggle have affected the Chinese people since the establishment of the People's Republic of China in 1949.

685. Loescher, Gil, with Ann Dull Loescher. *The Chinese way : life in the People's Republic of China*. New York : Harcourt, 1974. 206 p.
The authors visited China in 1971 and 1973, and are sympathetic to what they saw and heard in China.

686. Madsen, Richard. *Morality and power in a Chinese village*. Berkeley : University of California Press, 1984. 200 p.
Focuses on village controversies over local political leadership in the 1960s and 1970s. It offers insights about the aspect of Chinese life during the Cultural Revolution and the aftermath.

687. Sidel, Ruth. *Families of Fengsheng : urban life in China*. Baltimore, MD : Penguin, 1974. 166 p.
Personal observations of neighborhood life in China's cities during the Cultural Revolution. Describes neighborhood committees, factories, labor relations, health care, the role of women and senior citizens, and others.

688. Sidel, Ruth. *Revolutionary China : people, politics, and ping-pong*. New York : Delacorte Press, 1974. 178 p.

689. Watson, Andrew. *Living in China*. Totowa, NJ : Rowman & Littlefield, 1975. 192 p.
Contains information on various aspects of Chinese life in the Cultural Revolution. The author taught English for two years at the Xi'an Foreign Language Institute in the late 1960s.

690. White, Gordon. *The politics of class and class origin : the case of the Cultural Revolution*. Canberra : Australian National University : distributed by Contemporary China Centre, 1976. 97 p.

691. Whyte, Martin King and William L. Parish. *Urban life in contemporary China*. Chicago : University of Chicago Press, 1984. 408 p.

692.   Yu Chieh-hua. *The effects of Communist cultural revolution upon the political and social life of the people in the Chinese mainland.* Thesis (M.A. in Political Science). University of Manila, 1970. 128 leaves.

L. TRAVEL AND TOURISM

693.   Alley, Rewi. *Travels in China, 1966-1971.* 1st ed. Peking : New World Press, 1973. 588 p.
Based largely on author's notes of travels during the period of 1966-71. Most of the travels were made to people's communes, organizations, and other units which were considered to be models for work at that particular stage of the Cultural Revolution.

694.   *China travel : Shanghai, Hangzhou, Nanjing, Wuxi, Suzhou.* Beijing : China Travel and Tourism Press, 1975. 110 p.

695.   *China travel guide.* Peking : Cartographic Publishing House, 1974. 49 p.

696.   Terrill, Ross. *Flowers on an iron tree : five cities of China.* Boston : Little Brown, 1975. 423 p.
A report of author's visit to Shanghai, Dalian, Hangzhou, Wuhan, and Beijing in 1973.

M. MEDIA AND COMMUNICATION

697.   *Carry the great revolution on the journalistic front through to the end : repudiating the counter-revolutionary revisionist line on journalism of China's Khrushchov.* Peking : Foreign Languages Press, 1969. 63 p.
An editorial of Renmin Ribao, Hongqi, and Jiefangjun Bao.

698.   Chang Man. *The People's daily and the Red Flag magazine during the cultural revolution.* Hong Kong : Union Research Institute, c1969. 126 p.

699.   Chang, Won Ho. *Mass media in China : the history and the future.* 1st ed. Ames : Iowa State University Press, 1989. 308 p.
Consists of three parts: Part one describes the historical development of the Chinese media. Part two deals with the structure and function of major media organizations and includes content analyses of programs

and publications. Part three discusses journalism education and the role of the Chinese mass media.

700.   Hao Xiaoming. *Time magazine and the Chinese Cultural Revolution, 1966-1976 : a content analysis.* Thesis (M.A.). University of Missouri-Columbia. 1990. 140 leaves.

701.   Liu, Alan P. L. *Communications and national integration in communist China.* Berkeley : University of California Press, 1971. 225 p.

702.   Yuan Weiping. *A historical study of China's Cultural Revolution and its coverage by the New York Times.* Thesis (M.S.). Oklahoma State University, 1989. 79 leaves.

703.   Zhao Yongchang. *China's Great Cultural Revolution and its communication structure.* Thesis (M.A.). University of Hawaii at Manoa, 1994. 174 leaves.

N. ARCHAEOLOGY AND ART

704.   Chang, Arnold. *Painting in the People's Republic of China : the politics of style.* Boulder, CO : Westview Press, 1980. 130 p.
Serves as a useful summary of Chinese painting for the period of 1949-1980. Discusses the major issues that had influenced the Chinese art. Focuses on the art of three specialists (Guan Shanyue, Li Keran, and Qian Songyan) and traces their artistic careers since 1949.

705.   *Chinese arts and crafts.* Peking : Light Industry Publishing House ; Foreign Languages Press, 1973. 1 v.

706.   Cohen, Joan Lebold. *The new Chinese painting, 1949-1986.* New York : H. N. Abrams, 1987. 167 p.

707.   *Cultural relics unearthed during the period of the Great Cultural Revolution.* San Francisco : China Books, 1972. 15 p., 152 p. of plates. Text in English and Chinese.

708.   Galikowski, Maria. *Art and politics in China, 1949-1984.* Hong Kong : Chinese University Press, 1998. 289 p.
Discusses the major stages of development in Chinese art after 1949, and highlights the extent to which art was utilized as an integral component

of the Communist Party's socialist program. Traces the various phases of repression and liberalization that were a marked feature of China's post-1949 political and cultural scenes, including those chaotic years of the Cultural Revolution.

709. *Graphic art by workers in Shanghai, Yangchuan and Luta.* Peking : Foreign Languages Press, 1976. 71 p.
Selection of items from a 1974 exhibition of graphic art in Beijing.

710. Kraus, Richard Curt. *Brushes with power : modern politics and the Chinese art of calligraphy.* Berkeley : University of California Press, 1991. 208 p.

711. Laing, Ellen Johnston. *The winking owl : art in the People's Republic of China.* Berkeley ; Los Angeles : University of California Press, 1988. 194 p.
A survey of the principal genres of post-liberation art and the major issues that have governed artistic production. Consists of nine topical chapters about Chinese art between 1949 and 1976. Brief biographies of Chinese artists are included.

712. *Mao's graphic voice : pictorial posters from the Cultural Revolution.* Madison, WI : Elvehjem Museum of Art, 1996. 14 p.
A catalog of an exhibition (from a private collection in Shanghai) at the Elvehjem Museum of Art, Madison, Wisconsin, August 31-October 27, 1996.

713. *New archaeological finds in China : discoveries during the Cultural Revolution.* Peking : Foreign Languages Press, 1972-1978. 2 v.

714. *New archaeological finds in China : discoveries during the Cultural Revolution.* Revised 2nd ed. Peking : Foreign Languages Press, 1973. 72 p.
Contents include: Archaeological work during the Cultural Revolution; Han tombs at Mancheng; Tatu, the Yuan capital; Finds from Kansu; Chu tomb and weapons from Changsha; Perfect preservation after 2,100 years; More finds along the Silk Road; Tomb of the Ming Prince of Lu; The masses support archaeological work.

715. *Peasant paintings from Huhsien County.* Peking : Foreign Languages Press, 1974. 75 p.
Translation of: Hu Xian nong min hua xuan ji.

716. Sullivan, Michael. *Art and artists of twentieth-century China.* Berkeley, CA : University of California Press, 1996. 354 p.
A special discussion on the Cultural Revolution is in section 15 (p. 151-159).

717. Wilkinson, Endymion. *The people's comic book : red women's detachment and other Chinese comics.* New York : Doubleday, 1973. 156 p.
Seven comics in this book are cartoon renderings of popular films, plays, and novels in China including "Hong se niang zi jun."

718. Wilkinson, Endymion. *Translation of the People's comic book.* New York : Anchor Press, 1973. 272 p.
A selection of Chinese comics with the Chinese captions translated into English.

O. LANGUAGE AND LITERATURE

719. Bei Dao and others; Tony Barnstone, ed. *Out of the howling storm : the new Chinese poetry.* Middletown, CT : Wesleyan University Press ; Hanover, NH : University Press of New England, 1993. 155 p.
Contains works by Bei Dao, Yang Lian, Shu Ting, Jiang He, Gu Cheng, Duoduo, Zhang Zhen, Tang Yaping, Bei Ling, and others.

720. Bergman, Par. *Paragons of virtue in Chinese short stories during the Cultural Revolution.* Stockholm : P. Bergman, 1984. 215 p.
A study of "model stories" and exemplary persons in China with special emphasis on the Cultural Revolution period (up until the the year 1971-1972).

721. Chang Hsin-cheng. *Evening chats at Yenshang ; or, the case of Teng To.* Berkeley : Center for Chinese Studies, University of California, 1970. 56 p.

722. Chang Hsin-cheng. *The little red book and current Chinese language.* Berkeley : Center for Chinese Studies, University of California, 1968. 58 p.
A study of Mao Zedong's linguistic style as exemplified in "Quotations from Chairman Mao Tse-tung." It is Monograph no. 13 of the series "Studies in Chinese Communist Terminology."

723.   Chen Ruoxi. *The execution of Mayor Yin and other stories from the Great Proletarian Cultural Revolution*. Bloomington : Indiana University Press, 1978. 220 p.
A collection of eight short stories reflecting author's experience in the Cultural Revolution (1966-1973).
Contents include: The execution of Mayor Yin; Chairman Mao is a rotten egg; Night duty; Residency check; Jen Hsiu-lan; The big fish; Keng Erh in Peking; and Nixon's press corps.

724.   *City cousin, and other stories*. Peking : Foreign Languages Press, 1973. 124 p.
Contents include: City cousin; Look far, fly far; The call; Spring comes to a fishing village; The ferry at Billows Harbour; A shoulder pole; When the persimmons ripened; Home leave.

725.   Duoduo. *Looking out from death : from the Cultural Revolution to Tiananmen Square : the new Chinese poetry of Duoduo*. London : Bloomsbury, 1989. 125 p.

726.   Hao Ran. *Bright clouds*. Peking : Foreign Languages Press, 1974. 139 p.
Contents include: The lean chestnut horse; Shepherd's apprentice; Sending in vegetable seed; Visit on a snowy night; Bright clouds; Rain in Apricot Blossom Village; Honeymoon; Jade Spring.

727.   Hao Ran. *The call of fledgling and other children's stories*. Peking : Foreign Languages Press, 1974. 57 p.
Contents include: The chirruping grasshopper; The speckled hen; Making snowmen; Children's library; The call of the fledgling.

728.   Hao Ran. *The golden road*. Beijing : Foreign Languages Press, 1981. 390 p.
Translation of: Jin guang da dao, which was first published in China in 1972.

729.   He Dong. *Ask the sun*. 1st ed. Seattle, WA : Women in Translation, 1997. 99 p.
Short stories. Translation of: Spor solen.

730.   Hsu, Kai-yu. *The Chinese literary scene : a writer's visit to the People's Republic of China*. New York : Vintage Books, 1975. 267 p.

Reports of the result of a six-month visit to China in 1973 by the author. About half of the book consists of reports on author's interviews, and the other half consists of translations of poems, fictions, and criticism.

731.   Hsu, Kai-yu and Ting Wang, comp. *Literature of the People's Republic of China*. Bloomington, IN : Indiana University Press, 1980. 976 p.
The readings are selected and organized in relation to the major controversies that have shaken the politico-literary scene in China since 1949. Includes a chronology of major events relevant to the development of contemporary Chinese literature, a glossary of Chinese special terms, and a list of Chinese references.

732.   Jin Ha. *Ocean of words : army stories*. Cambridge, MA : Zoland Books, 1996. 205 p.
A collection of stories to describe the People's Liberation Army soldiers and officers' life on the Chinese-Russian border in the 1970s.

733.   Kao, George, ed. *Two writers and the Cultural Revolution : Lao She and Chen Jo-hsi*. Hong Kong : Chinese University Press, 1980. 212 p.
Includes Lao She's pre-1949 output and Chen Ruoxi (Chen Jo-hsi)'s writings in English and/or Chinese, together with essays about the two writers.

734.   King, Richard. *A shattered mirror : the literature of the Cultural Revolution*. Thesis (Ph.D.). University of British Columbia, 1984. 391 leaves.

735.   Leung, Laifong. *Morning sun : interviews with post-Mao Chinese writers*. Armonk, NY : M.E. Sharpe, 1994. 392 p.
A collection of interviews with 26 young writers who participated and/or suffered in the Cultural Revolution. The social, political, and cultural milieu of the period emerged in detail. Contents include: Appendix A: Chronology of important events since 1949; Appendix B: Political and other terms.

736.   Li Bihua. *Farewell to my concubine : a novel*. New York : W. Morrow, c1993. 255 p.
A story that spans more than 50 years in the lives of two men at the Peking opera. Also an absorbing drama of the period in Chinese modern history from the warlord era through the Cultural Revolution.
Translation of: Ba wang bie ji. Author's name on the book: Lilian Lee.

737. Li Ruqing. *Island militia women*. 1st ed. Peking : Foreign Languages Press, 1975. 296 p.
      Translation of: Hai dao nu min bin.

738. Li Xintian. *Bright red star : story*. 1st ed. Peking : Foreign Languages Press, 1974. 142 p.
      Translation of: Shan shan de hong xing.

739. Li Ying. *Mountains crimsoned with flowers*. Peking : Foreign Languages Press, 1974. 32 p.
      Translation of sixteen poems from "Hong hua man shan."

740. Liu So-la. *Chaos and all that*. Honolulu : University of Hawaii Press, 1994. 134 p.
      Translation of: Hun dun jia li ge leng.
      Describes the inner life of novel's leading character, Huang Haha. Contains recollections of childhood, pet ownership, and marriage with discussions of art, sex, and murder.

741. Liu Xuemin. *Poetry as modernization : "misty poetry" of the cultural revolution*. Thesis (Ph.D.). University of California, Berkeley, 1992. 233 leaves.

742. Liu Zongren. *Six Tanyin Alley*. San Francisco : China Books & Periodicals, 1989. 313 p.

743. Lu Xinhua et al. *Wounded : new stories of the Cultural Revolution, 77-78*. Hong Kong : Joint Publishing Co., 1979. 220 p.

744. Ma Bo. *Blood red sunset : a memoir of the Chinese Cultural Revolution*. New York : Penguin, 1996. 371 p.
      Previously published: New York : Viking, 1995. Translation of: Xue se huang hun.
      It is a story of a young man who joined the revolution in rural northern China in the Cultural Revolution. There he participated in the activities to re-educate herd owners and "capitalist Chinese." Then, after casually criticizing a Chinese leader, he was betrayed by his friends, beaten, and imprisoned.

745. Mao Zedong. *Definitive translation of Mao Tse-tung on literature and art : the cultural revolution in context*. Washington, DC : Alwhite Publication, 1967. 43 p.

Edited by Thomas N. White.

746.   Mao Zedong. *Mao Tsetung poems*. Peking : Foreign Languages Press, 1976. 105 p.
Chinese and English on opposite pages.

747.   Maxwell, Stanley M. *The man who couldn't be killed : an incredible story of faith and courage during China's cultural revolution*. Boise, ID : Pacific Press Publishing Association, 1995. 222 p.

748.   McDougall, Bonnies S. and Paul Clark. *Popular Chinese Literature and performing arts in the People's Republic of China, 1949-1979*. Berkeley : University of California Press, 1984. 341 p.
Based on papers presented at a workshop held at Harvard University in June 1979.

749.   Peng, Jia-Lin. *Wild cat : stories of the Cultural Revolution*. Dunvegan, Ontario : Cormorant Books, 1990. 180 p.

750.   Perry, Elizabeth J. and Li Xun. *Revolutionary rudeness : the language of Red Guards and rebel workers in China's Cultural Revolution*. Bloomington : East Asian Studies Center, Indiana University, 1993. 31 p.

751.   *Seeds and other stories*. Peking : Foreign Languages Press, 1972. 193 p.
Contents include: Red Cliff revisited; A night in "Potato" Village; Half the population; Raiser of sprouts; Third time to school; The case of the missing ducks; A detour to Dragon Village; Raising seedlings; Selling rice; Two ears of rice; Crossing Chungchou Dam.

752.   *Story of the modern ballet : Red detachment of women*. Peking : Foreign Languages Press, 1973. 39 p.
Story and plots of Hong se niang zi jun.

753.   Wang Shuyuan. *Azalea mountain : a revolutionary modern Peking opera*. Peking : Foreign Languages Press, 1974. 128 p.
Also includes short stories and poems by various authors.

754.   Yang Lan. *Chinese fiction of the Cultural Revolution*. Hong Kong : Hong Kong University Press, 1998. 340 p.

755. Yang Xiao. *The making of a peasant doctor*. Peking : Foreign Languages Press ; London : Mao Tse-tung Memorial Centre, 1976. 199 p.
Translation of: Hong yu.

756. Yang Xiao-ming. *The rhetoric of propaganda : a tagmemic analysis of selected documents of the Cultural Revolution of China*. New York : Peter Lang, c1994. 138 p.
An analysis of the propaganda discourse, with a general discussion of some characteristics of Chinese propaganda during the Cultural Revolution. The results of the study indicate that the tagmemic approach to language is a workable model for textual analysis.

757. *Young pathbreaker and other stories*. Peking : Foreign Languages Press, 1975. 178 p.
Translation of: Xiao jiang and other stories.
Contents include: Out to learn; Women forge workers; The sharp cutter edge; A young pathbreaker; A screw; Hidden reef; Morning sun; Pupil excels master; Re-examination; A steel worker's assistant.

758. *Young skipper : and other stories*. Peking : Foreign Languages Press, 1973. 97 p.
Translation of: Xin lai de lao da.
Contents include: The Young skipper; Old sentry; Old Hsin's day of retirement; Red navigation route.

759. Yu Hua. *The past and the punishments*. Honolulu : University of Hawaii Press, 1996. 277 p.
A collection of short stories, which take on a haunting and harrowing journey from classical China through the Cultural Revolution and into the new era of economic reform.

760. Yu, Shiao-Ling. *The cultural revolution in post-Mao literature*. Thesis (Ph.D.). University of Wisconsin--Madison, 1983. 336 leaves.
A study of the impact of the Cultural Revolution on the lives of the Chinese people as reflected in the fiction, poetry, and dramatic literature produced during 1977-1978.

761. Zhang, Song Nan. *Cowboy on the steppes*. Toronto, Ontario ; Plattsburgh, NY : Tundra Books, 1997. 32 p.

762. Zhang Xianliang. *Grass soup.* 1st American ed. Boston : D.R. Godine, 1995. 247 p.
      Translation of: Fan nao jiu shi zhi hui.

763. Zhang Xianliang. *Half of man is woman.* London ; New York : Viking, 1988. 252 p.
      Translation of: Nan ren de yi ban shi nu ren.

764. Zhang Yongmei. *Battle of the Hsisha Archipelago : reportage in verse.* Peking : Foreign Languages Press, 1975. 33 p.
      A description of a battle on the South China Sea Islands.

P. MUSIC, FILM, DRAMA, THEATER, AND SPORTS

765. *Azalea Mountain : a modern revolutionary Peking opera.* September 1973 script of the Peking Opera Troupe of Peking. Peking : Foreign Languages Press, 1976. 63 p.
      Opera.
      Libretto of Du juan shan.

766. Chin, Luke Kai-hsin. *The politics of drama reform in China after 1949 : elite strategy of resocialization.* Thesis (Ph.D.). New York University, 1980. 326 leaves.

767. China Ballet Troupe. *Red detachment of women : a modern revolutionary ballet.* May 1970 script. Peking : Foreign Languages Press, 1972. 169 p.
      Ballet scenario and music scores of Hong se niang zi jun.

768. Clark, Paul. *Chinese cinema : culture and politics since 1949.* New York : Cambridge University Press, 1987. 243 p.
      Covers the Chinese films produced by the Left from the 1930s until 1984. The chapters are essentially chronological, including the chapter "Cultural Revolution, 1964-1978."

769. Fan-Long, Grace. *A study of idiomatic piano compositions during the cultural revolution in the People's Republic of China.* Thesis (D.M.A.). University of North Texas, 1991. 47 leaves.
      Text of a lecture recital presented on June 3, 1991 at the University of North Texas.

770. Howard, Roger. *Contemporary Chinese theatre*. London : Heinemann Educational, 1978. 138 p.
Consists of two parts: the first part gives a brief historical background on Chinese drama up to 1949, and the second part traces the development of some classifications of drama since 1949. Discusses topics including the period before the Cultural Revolution, the Cultural Revolution, new workers and peasants' amateur theater, and the productions of the professionals.

771. Howard, Roger. *The tragedy of Mao in the Lin Piao Period and other plays*. Colchester : Theatre Action Press, 1989. 132 p.
Contents include: The tragedy of Mao in the Lin Piao Period; Margery Kempe; White sea; Queen.

772. Jiang Qing. *On the revolution of Peking opera*. Peking : Foreign Languages Press, 1968. 64 p.
Translation of: Tan Jing ju ge ming.

773. Kraus, Richard Curt. *Pianos and politics in China : middle-class ambitions and the struggle over Western music*. New York : Oxford University Press, 1989. 288 p.
Biographies of notable modern Chinese composers and musicians, including Xian Xinghai, Fu Cong, Yin Chengzong, Liu Shikun, Li Jiefu, He Luting, and Yu Huiyong (cultural minister in 1970s). Provides a relatively full picture of Chinese politics on music from 1949 to 1989 especially during the Cultural Revolution period.

774. *Little sisters of the grassland*. Peking : Foreign Languages Press, 1973. 89 p.
A scenario.

775. MacKerras, Colin. *Performing arts in contemporary China*. London : Routledge and Kegan Paul, 1981. 243 p.

776. Mowry, Hua-yuan Li. *Yang-pan hsi--New theater in China*. Berkeley : Center for Chinese Studies, University of California, 1973. 117 p.
This work is the No. 15 of the series "Studies in Chinese Communist Terminology."

777. Peking Opera Troupe of Shanghai. *On the docks : a modern revolutionary Peking opera*. January 1972 script. Peking : Foreign Languages Press, 1973. 41 p.

Opera.
Libretto of Hai gang.

778.   Ong, Henry. *Madame Mao's memories : a play.* Washington, DC : Three Continents Press, 1992. 43 p.

779.   *Raid on the White Tiger Regiment.* September 1972 script. Peking : Foreign Languages Press, 1973. 54 p.
Reprinted from *Chinese literature,* 1973, v. 3.
Libretto of Qi xi Bai hu tuan.

780.   Revolutionary Literary and Art Fighters of the Central Philharmonic Society and China Peking Opera Troupe. *Piano music the Red lantern : with Peking Opera singing, selected songs.* Peking : Chinese Literature, 1968. 32 p.
Jointly created by the Revolutionary Literary and Art Fighters of the Central Philharmonic Society and China Peking Opera Troupe ; piano music by Yin Chengzong. Chinese words with romanization; English translation follows each song.
Contents include: I am filled with courage and strength; My spirit storms the sky; Hatred in my heart sprouts a hundredfold.

781.   *Red lantern : modern revolutionary Peking opera.* Peking : Foreign Languages Press, 1972. 98 p.
Libretto of Hong deng ji.

782.   *Revolutionary songs of China.* Peking : Foreign Languages Press, 1971. music (4 folders).
Contents include: The east is red; Sailing the seas depends on the helmsman; The three main rules of discipline and the eight points for attention; Singing of the socialist motherland.

783.   *Shachiapang : a modern revolutionary Peking opera.* May 1970 script. Peking : Foreign Languages Press, 1972. 101 p.
Opera.
Libretto of Sha jia bang.

784.   Shen, Bright. *H'un = Lacerations = Hen : in memoriam 1966-1976 : for orchestra.* New York : G. Schirmer ; Milwaukee, WI : Distributed by H. Leonard Corp., 1995, c1988. 1 score (59 p.).
Orchestra music.

785. Snow, Lois Wheeler. *China on stage : an American actress in the People's Republic.* New York : Random House, 1972. 328 p.
A detailed discussion of revolutionary model operas and ballets. Contains the full text of three revolutionary operas: Taking Tiger Mountain by strategy, Shajiabang, and The red lantern. Also contains one ballet: Red detachment of women.

786. "Song of the Dragon River" Group of Shanghai. *Song of the Dragon River : a modern revolutionary Peking Opera.* January 1972 script. Peking : Foreign Languages Press, 1972. 43 p.
Opera.
Libretto of Long jiang song.

787. *Sports in China.* Peking : Foreign Languages Press, 1973. 95 p.

788. *Taking the bandits' stronghold : modern Peking opera on contemporary revolutionary theme.* Colombo : Afro-Asian Writers' Bureau, 1967. 68 p.
Libretto of Zhi qu Wei hu shan.

789. *Taking Tiger Mountain by strategy : a modern revolutionary Peking opera.* July 1970 script. Peking : Foreign Languages Press, 1971. 113 p.
Revised collectively by the "Taking Tiger by Strategy" Group of the Peking Opera Troupe of Shanghai.
Libretto of Zhi qu Wei hu shan.

790. *To find men truly great and noble-hearted we must look here in the present : in praise of the modern revolutionary Peking opera, Taking Tiger Mountain by Strategy.* Peking : Foreign Languages Press, 1971. 68 p.

791. *Unity and friendship : the Asian-African-Latin American Table-tennis Friendship Invitational Tournament.* Peking : Foreign Languages Press, 1973. 80 p.

792. *Vicious motive, despicable tricks : a criticism of M. Antonioni's anti-China film.* Peking : Foreign Languages Press, 1974. 18 p.
An article written by the Renmin Ribao commentator to criticize Michelangelo Antonioni's film "La Cina."

793. Wang Yuanjian. *Sparkling red star (film scenario) : an adaptation by the Chinese People's Liberation Army August First Film Studio from the*

novel of the same title by Li Hsin-tien. Peking : Foreign Languages Press, 1976. 75 p.
Translation of: Shan shan de hong xing.

794. Wong, Cynthia P. *The east is red : musicians and politics of the Chinese Cultural Revolution, 1966-1976*. Thesis (M.M.). Florida State University, 1993. 252 leaves.

795. Zhang Yongmei et al. *Fighting on the plain : a modern revolutionary Peking opera*. July 1973 script. Peking : Foreign Languages Press, 1976. 44 p.
Opera. Written by Zhang Yongmei and other members of the China Peking Opera Troupe
Libretto of Ping yuan zuo zhan.

VI

Biographies, Memoirs, and Firsthand Observations

A. BIOGRAPHIES

1. Mao Zedong and His Works

796. Brugger, Bill. *China : radicalism to revisionism, 1962-1979.* London : Croom helm, 1981. 275 p.
Examines the way in which Mao Zedong governed and the fluctuations in his attitude.

797. Chang Hsin-cheng. *The little red book and current Chinese language.* Berkeley : Center for Chinese Studies, University of California, 1968. 58 p.
A study of Mao Zedong's linguistic style as exemplified in "Quotations from Chairman Mao Tse-tung." It is the Monograph no. 13 of the series "Studies in Chinese Communist Terminology."

798. *Eternal glory to the great leader and teacher Chairman Mao Tsetung.* Peking : Foreign Languages Press, 1976. 40 p.
Contents include: Message to the whole party, the whole army, and the people of all nationalities throughout the country; Memorial speech; Decision on the establishment of a memorial hall for the great leader and teacher Chairman Mao Tsetung.

799. Fitzgerald, C. P. (Charles Patrick). *Mao Tse-tung and China.* Harmonsworth, England : New York : Penguin Books, 1977. 197 p.
A biography of Mao Zedong covering his entire life.

800. *Great leader Chairman Mao will live forever in our hearts.* Peking : s.n., 1976. 65 p.
      On back cover: September 20, 1976.

801. Hammond, Edward. *To embrace the moon : an illustrated biography of Mao Zedong.* New York : Lancaster-Miller Publishers, 1980. 192 p.

802. Han, Suyin. *Wind in the tower : Mao Tse-tung and the Chinese revolution, 1949-1975.* London : Cape, 1976. 404 p.
      This is the second volume of author's biography of Mao Tse-tung. The first volume is entitled *"The morning deluge : Mao Tse-tung and the Chinese revolution, 1893-1953."* The second part of this volume is about "The Cultural Revolution and After," which focuses on Mao's ideas, writings, and speeches during the Cultural Revolution.

803. Hawkins, John N. *Mao Tse-tung and education : his thought and teachings.* Hamden, CT : Linnet Books, 1974. 260 p.
      Examines Mao's analysis of the basic aims, goals and principles of education, as well as problems related to education.

804. Hollingworth, Clare. *Mao and the men against him.* London : Jonathan Cape Ltd., 1985. 372 p.
      Studies on Mao Zedong's political struggles, particularly in the Cultural Revolution.

805. Karnow, Stanley. *Mao and China : a legacy of turmoil.* 3rd ed., revised and updated. New York : Penguin Books, 1990. 573 p.
      An incisive and updated observation combines with a new introduction to provide a better understanding of those events during the Cultural Revolution and the aftermath including 1989 Tiananmen Square incident.

806. Karnow, Stanley. *Mao and China : from revolution to revolution.* New York : Viking Press, 1972. 592 p.
      A description of the course of the Cultural Revolution, the debates and struggles among Chinese leaders in the 1960s, and the central role played by Mao Zedong.

807. Karnow, Stanley. *Mao and China : inside China's cultural revolution.* New York : Viking Press, 1984. 592 p.
      Originally published: New York : Viking Press, 1972.

808. Lawrance, Alan. *Mao Zedong : a bibliography*. New York : Greenwood Press, 1991. 197 p.
Comprises entries of books and journal articles published in English plus some important works in other languages, including Mao Zedong's works, biographies, and other works covering Mao's life and Mao's era.

809. Li Zhisui; editorial assistance of Anne F. Thurston. *The private life of Chairman Mao : the memoirs of Mao's personal physician*. New York : Random House, 1994. 682 p.
Memoirs of Mao's physician who was with Mao from 1954 to 1976.

810. Lifton, Robert Jay. *Revolutionary immortality : Mao Tse-tung and the Chinese cultural revolution*. New York : Norton, 1976. 178 p.

811. MacFarquhar, Emily. *China : Mao's last leap*. London : Economist Newspapers, 1968. 26 p.

812. Mao Zedong. *Chairman talks to the people ; talks and letters : 1956-1971*. 1st American ed. New York : Pantheon Books, 1975. 352 p.
Edited by Stuart Schram.

813. Mao Zedong. *Mao papers*. London ; New York : Oxford University Press, 1970. 221 p.
A selection of writings not included in Mao's Selected Works. Includes letters, speeches and instructions by Mao Zedong during the Cultural Revolution. Also consists of a chronological bibliography of Mao's writings in English and Chinese including those not translated into English. Anthology and bibliography edited by Jerome Chen.

814. Mao Zedong. *Mao Tse-tung and Lin Piao : post-revolutionary writings*. Garden City, NY : Doubleday, 1972. 536 p.
Contains writings of Mao Zedong and Lin Biao written since 1949. The appendix includes two documents: the Decision of the Central Committee of the Chinese Communist Party concerning the Great Proletarian Cultural Revolution (Sixteen Points), and the Constitution of the Communist Party of China (adopted in 1969).

815. Mao Zedong. *Mao Tse-tung unrehearsed : talks and letters, 1956-71*. Harmondsworth, Middlesex, England : Penguin, 1974. 352 p.
Consists of twenty-six statements, speeches, and articles which were published on Red Guard publications during the Cultural Revolution. Edited by Stuart Schram.

816.   Mao Zedong. *Mao Tse-tung's quotations : the Red Guard's handbook.*
        Nashville : International Center, George Peabody College for Teachers,
        1967. 311 p.
        The quotations are from the original English language edition published
        in Beijing in 1966.

817.   Mao Zedong. *Quotations from Chairman Mao Tse-tung.* 1st ed. Peking :
        Foreign Languages Press, 1966. 311 p.
        Translation of: Mao zhu xi yu lu.

818.   Mao Zedong. *Quotations from Chairman Mao Tse-tung.* New York :
        Bantam Books, 1967. 179 p.
        Translation of: Mao zhu xi yu lu.

819.   Mao Zedong. *Quotations from Chairman Mao Tse-tung.* New York :
        Praeger, 1967. 182 p.
        Translation of: Mao zhu xi yu lu. Edited by Stuart R. Schram.

820.   Mao Zedong. *Writings of Mao Zedong, 1949-1976.* Armonk, NY : M.E.
        Sharpe, 1986- (2 v. published)
        This multi-volume edition features a new translation and full
        annotations, including complete information on all known Chinese and
        Western sources. Edited by Michael Y. W. Kau and John Leung.

821.   Michael, Franz H. *Mao and the perpetual revolution : an illuminating
        study of Mao Tse-tung's role in China and world communism.*
        Woodbury, NY : Barron's, 1977. 326 p.
        A review of more than half a century of revolutionary activity in China,
        with close attention to the role of Mao Zedong and other Chinese
        Communist Party leaders.

822.   Morrison, Joe and Jonathan Unger, ed. *Mao Zedong and the cultural
        revolution.* New York : M.E. Sharp, 1985. 99 p.

823.   Rice, Edward E. *Mao's way.* Berkeley : University of California Press,
        1972. 596 p.
        This work aims to study Mao Zedong's personality and character, from
        his childhood to 1970. Half of the book deals with the period of 1965-
        1970. The author served as an American Consul General in Hong Kong
        during the Cultural Revolution. It was written after his return to the
        United States.

824. Salisbury, Harrison Evans. *The new emperors : China in the era of Mao and Deng.* Boston : Little, Brown, 1992. 544 p.
Provides a detailed picture of the personal relationships and private lives of China's highest officers of the past 40 years.

825. Schram, Stuart R. *Mao Zedong, a preliminary reassessment.* Hong Kong : The Chinese University Press, 1983. 104 p.
Contains author's three lectures given at the United College in 1982. Includes: The formative years, 1917-1937; A quarter century of achievements, 1937-1962; The final phase: from apotheosis to oblivion.

826. Schram, Stuart R. *The thought of Mao Tse-tung.* New York : Cambridge University Press, 1989. 242 p.

827. Sherman, James C. *Mao Tse-tung's concept of higher education.* Thesis (Ph.D.). University of Denver, Colorado. 177 leaves.

828. Starr, John Bryan. *Continuing the revolution : the political thought of Mao.* Princeton, NJ : Princeton University Press, 1979. 366 p.
Explicates Mao Zedong's political thought by investigating its internal logic and evolution. Relates major shifts in Mao's ideas to the events that influenced those shifts.

829. Starr, John Bryan and Nancy Anne Dyer, comps. *Post-liberation works of Mao Zedong : a bibliography and index.* Berkeley : Center for Chinese Studies, University of California, Berkeley, 1976. 222 p.
A chronologically arranged listing of 797 items of Mao's post-1949 works available in English.

830. Terrill, Ross. *Mao : a biography.* 1st ed. New York : Harper & Row, 1980. 481 p.
A chronological account of Mao Zedong's career. Nearly one-third of the book is devoted to Mao's last decade, the Cultural Revolution period.

831. Terrill, Ross. *Mao : a biography.* Australian ed. Sydney, NSW : Hale & Iremonger, 1995. 524 p.

832. Wagemann, Mildred Lina Ellen. *The changing image of Mao Tse-tung : leadership image and social structure.* Thesis (Ph.D.). Cornell University, 1974. 175 leaves.
Examines Mao's position and image during the Cultural Revolution as well as the social structural changes in progress since 1949.

833.   Wang Xizhe. *Mao Zedong and the Cultural Revolution.* Kowloon, Hong Kong : Plough Publications, 1981. 79 p.

834.   Wilson, Dick, ed. *Mao Tse-tung in the scales of history : a preliminary assessment.* Cambridge, England ; New York : Cambridge University Press, 1977. 331 p.

2. Liu Shaoqi and His Works

835.   *Betrayal of proletarian dictatorship is the heart of the book of "Self-cultivation."* Peking : Foreign Languages Press, 1967. 13 p.
Translation of: Xiu yang de yao hai shi bei pan wu chan jie ji zhuan zheng.

836.   Chen Yung-ping. *Chinese political thought : Mao Tse-tung and Liu Shaochi.* Revised ed. The Hague : Martinus Nijhoff, 1971. 129 p.
Examines the fundamentals of Chinese Communist ideology, and the disagreements between Mao Zedong and Liu Shaoqi.

837.   Dittmer, Lowell. *Liu Shao-chi and the Chinese cultural revolution : the politics of mass criticism.* Berkeley : University of California Press, 1974. 386 p.

838.   Dittmer, Lowell. *Liu Shaoqi and the Chinese Cultural Revolution.* Revised ed. Armonk, NY : M.E. Sharpe, 1997. 382 p.

839.   Harman, Richard Snyder. *The Maoist case against Liu Shaochi (1967) : a leadership crisis in the Chinese People's Republic.* Thesis (Ph.D.). University of Virginia, 1969. 298 leaves.

840.   Kent, A. E. (Ann E.). *Indictment without trial : the case of Liu Shao-Ch'i.* Canberra : Department of International Relations, Research School of Pacific Studies, Institute of Advanced Studies, Australian National University, 1969. 68 p.

841.   Li Tien-min. *Liu Shao-ch'i : Mao's first heir-apparent.* Taipei : Institute of International Relations, 1975. 223 p.

842.   Liu Shaoqi. *Collected works of Liu Shao-chi.* Hong Kong : Union Research Institute, 1968-1969. 3 v.

Contents: v. 1. Before 1944. v. 2. 1945-1957. v. 3. 1958-1967. Three volumes comprise a total of 143 writings and speeches by Liu Shaoqi including "Self-examinations."

843.   O'keefe, Thomas E. *Liu Shao-chi : a political biography.* Thesis (Ph.D.). St. John's University, 1968. 239. leaves.

3. Zhou Enlai

844.   Archer, Jules. *Chou En-lai.* New York : Hawthorn Books, 1973. 198 p.

845.   Fang, Percy Jucheng and Lucy Guinong Fang. *Zhou Enlai : a profile.* 1st ed. Beijing : Foreign Languages Press : Distributed by China International Book Trading Corporation, 1986. 238 p.

846.   Hammond, Edward. *Coming of grace : an illustrated biography of Zhou Enlai.* New York : Lancaster Miller Publishers, 1980. 196 p.
Documents the life and career of Zhou Enlai.

847.   Han, Suyin. *Eldest son : Zhou Enlai and the making of modern China, 1898-1976.* 1st ed. New York : Hill and Wang, 1994. 483 p.
Based on a series of eleven interviews with Zhou Enlai, meetings with Zhou's wife Deng Yingchao, and other family members and colleagues, as well as unusual access to the Chinese Communist Party's archives, the author provides a useful overview of Zhou Enlai's life. It covers the violent excesses of the Cultural Revolution period and the diplomatic rapprochement with the West in the 1970s.

848.   Hsu, Kai-yu. *Chou En-lai : China's gray eminence.* 1st ed. Garden City, NY : Doubleday, 1968. 294 p.

849.   Keith, Ronald C. *The diplomacy of Zhou Enlai.* New York : St. Martin's Press, 1989. 268 p.

850.   Robinson, Thomas W. *Chou En-lai : a statement of his political "style," with comparisons with Mao Tse-tung and Lin Piao.* Santa Monica, CA : Rand Corp., 1970. 22 p.

851.   Roots, John McCook. *Chou : an informal biography of China's legendary Chou En-lai.* 1st ed. Garden City, NY : Doubleday, 1978. 220 p.

852. Shao Kuo-kang. *Zhou Enlai and the foundations of Chinese foreign policy*. New York : St. Martin's Press, 1996. 370 p.
A comprehensive survey of China's foreign relations from 1949-1976 focusing on the significant role Zhou Enlai played. It studies Chinese foreign relations with the United States, the Soviet Union, and the Third World countries, as well as Zhou Enlai's negotiating skills.

853. *We will always remember Premier Chou En-lai*. 1st ed. Peking : Foreign Languages Press, 1977. 196 p.

854. Wilson, Dick. *Chou, the story of Zhou Enlai, 1898-1976*. London : Hutchinson, 1984. 348 p.
Records Zhou's crucial role in the establishment of the People's Republic, the 1950s, the upheavals of the Cultural Revolution. and the diplomacy in the 1970s that led to China's rapprochement with the West.

855. Wilson, Dick. *Zhou Enlai : a biography*. 1st American ed. New York : Viking, 1984. 349 p.
Originally published in Great Britain under the title: *Chou, the story of Zhou Enlai 1898-1976*.

4. Lin Biao
see Lin Biao and Lin Biao Affair (III, Part B)

5. Deng Xiaoping and His Works

856. Chang, David W. *Zhou Enlai and Deng Xiaoping in the Chinese leadership succession crisis*. Lanham, MD : University Press of America, c1984. 386 p.

857. Chi Hsin (Research group). *Teng Hsiao-ping : a political biography*. Hong Kong : Cosmos Books ; New York : distributed in North America by Books New China, c1978. 271 p.
Includes a series of documents from the Chinese press.

858. Deng Xiaoping. *Deng Xiaoping : speeches and writings*. New York : Pergamon Press, 1984. 379 p.
Consists of speeches, talks, and writings given by Deng Xiaoping between 1956 and 1984.

859. Deng Xiaoping. *Selected works of Deng Xiaoping.* 1st ed. Beijing : Foreign Languages Press. 1984-1994. 3 v.
Contents: v. 1. 1938-1965. v. 2. 1975-1982. v. 3. 1982-1992.
Translation of: Deng Xiaoping wen xuan. Translated by the Bureau for the Compilation and Translation of Works of Marx, Lenin, and Stalin under the Central Committee of the Communist Party of China
In volume 3, eight speeches (1975) reflect the struggle Deng Xiaoping waged against the Gang of Four.

860. Deng Xiaoping. *Speeches and writings.* 1st ed. Oxford ; New York : Pergamon, 1984. 101 p.
A collection of speeches, writings, and talks given by Deng Xiaoping between 1956 and 1984.

861. Department for the Research on Party Literature, the Central Committee of the Chinese Communist Party and Xinhua News Agency, eds. *Deng Xiaoping.* 1st ed. Beijing : Central Party Literature Publishing House, 1988. 302 p.

862. Franz, Uli. *Deng Xiaoping.* 1st ed. Boston : Harcourt Brace Jovanovich, 1988. 340 p.
Translated from German.

863. Lee, Ching-hua. *Teng Hsiao-ping's political biography.* Thesis (Ph.D.). New York University, 1984. 344 leaves.

864. Lee, Ching-hua. *Deng Xiaoping : the Marxist road to the forbidden city.* Princeton, NJ : The Kingston Press, 1985. 254 p.
Records Deng's career through his early life to the Cultural Revolution and post-Mao reform movement.

865. Lubetkin, Wendy. *Deng Xiaoping.* New York : Chelsea House, 1988. 111 p.

866. Salisbury, Harrison Evans. *The new emperors : China in the era of Mao and Deng.* Boston : Little, Brown, 1992. 544 p.
Provides a detailed picture of the personal relationships and private lives of China's highest officers of the past 40 years.

867. Yang, Benjamin. *Deng : a political biography.* Armonk, NY : M.E. Sharpe, 1997. 250 p.

A political biography of Deng Xiaoping. Includes detailed accounts on high-level Chinese Communist Party politics, Deng's changing relations with his party colleagues, and his roles in the Chinese politics.

6. Jiang Qing

868. *Chiang Ching, Mao Tse-tung's wife.* Taipei : World Anti-Communist League, Asian Peoples' Anti-Communist League, 1973. 44, 6 p.

869. Chung, Hua-min and Arthur C. Miller. *Madame Mao : a profile of Chiang Ch'ing.* Hong Kong : Union Research Institute, 1968. 314 p.
An English edition of *Jiang Qing Zheng Zhuan,* which was originally published in 1967.

870. *Great trial in Chinese history : the trial of the Lin Biao and Jiang Qing counter-revolutionary cliques, Nov. 1980-Jan. 1981.* 1st ed. Beijing : New World Press ; Elmsford, NY : Distributed by Pergamon Press, 1981. 234 p.

871. Ly, Singko. *The fall of Madam Mao.* New York : Vantage Press, 1979. 136 p.

872. *Summary of the forum on the work in literature and art in the armed forces with which comrade Lin Piao entrusted comrade Chiang Ching.* Peking : Foreign Languages Press, 1968. 48 p.
Translation of: Lin Biao tong zhi wei tuo Jiang Qing tong zhi zhao kai de bu dui wen yi gong zuo zuo tan hui ji yao.

873. Tai, Dwan L. *Chiang Ching : the emergence of a revolutionary political leader.* 1st ed. Hicksville, NY : Exposition Press, 1974. 222 p.

874. Terrill, Ross. *Madame Mao : a white-boned demon : a biography of Madame Mao Zedong.* Touchstone 1st ed. New York : Simon & Schuster, 1992. 466 p.
Revised edition of: *The white-Boned Demon : a biography of Madame Mao.*

875. Terrill, Ross. *The White-Boned Demon : a biography of Madame Mao Zedong.* 1st ed. New York : W. Morrow & Co., 1984. 446 p.
An account of Jiang's life from her childhood to the trial. A biography captures both Jiang's astonishing life and turbulent personality.

876.   Witke, Roxane. *Comrade Chiang Ching.* 1st ed. Boston : Little, Brown, c1972. 549 p.
A detailed account of the life and career of Jiang Qing. Based largely on Jiang Qing's oral account, author's notes, and translations. The author had interviews with Jiang Qing in Beijing and Guangzhou in the summer of 1972.

7. Kang Sheng

877.   Anderson, Dennis J. *Kang Sheng : a political biography, 1924-1970.* Thesis (Ph.D.). St. John's University, 1973. 202 leaves.

878.   Byron, John and Robert Pack. *The claws of the dragon : Kang Sheng, the evil genius behind Mao and his legacy of terror in People's China.* New York : Simon & Schuster, c1992. 560 p.
A political biography of Kang Sheng, one of the most influential and sinister figures in modern China.

879.   Faligot, Roger and Remi Kauffer. *The Chinese secret service.* New York : Morrow, c1989. 527 p.
Translation of: Kang Sheng et les services secrets chinois.
Examines, in particular, the life and career of Kang Sheng and other Chinese intelligence officers. This work was also published in Great Britain in 1989 by Headline Book.

8. Zhang Chunqiao

880.   Walder, Andrew George. *Chang Ch'un-chiao and Shanghai's January Revolution.* Ann Arbor : Center for Chinese Studies, University of Michigan, 1978. 150 p.
Provides an interpretation of Shanghai's January Revolution in 1967 and Zhang Chunqiao's role in this event.

9. Yao Wenyuan

881.   Ragvald, Lars. *Yao Wenyuan as a literary critic and theorist : the emergency of Chinese Zhdanovism.* Thesis (Dr., Department of Oriental Languages). University of Stockholm, 1978. 225 p.

10. Wu Han

882.   Ansley, Clive M. (Clive Malcolm). *The heresy of Wu Han : his play "Hai Jui's dismissal" and its role in China's cultural revolution.* Toronto : University of Torono Press, c1971. 125 p.

883.   *Case of Wu Han in the Cultural Revolution.* White Plains, NY : International Arts and Sciences Press, 1969-1970. 5 parts.
Originally published in Chinese Studies in History and Philosophy, vol. 2, no. 1 & 3; vol. 3, no. 1-3.

884.   Gray, Jack and Patrick Cavendish. *Chinese communism in crisis : Maoism and the cultural revolution.* New York : Praeger, 1968. 279 p.
Studies the major events and issues of the 1966-1967 crisis in China. The main sources used in this work are from Red Guard posters, pamphlets, and newspapers. The appendix, approximately half the book, contains twelve documentary sources including Wu Han's *the Dismissal of Hai Jui.* Yao Wenyuan's *On the new historical drama--the Dismissal of Hai Jui,* and other articles.

885.   Mazur, Mary Gale. *A man of his times : Wu Han, the historian.* Thesis (Ph.D.). University of Chicago, 1993. 688 leaves.

886.   Pusey, James R. *Wu Han : attacking the present through the past.* Cambridge : East Asian Research Center, Harvard University Press, 1969. 84 p.

11. Zhou Yang

887.   *To trumpet bourgeois literature and art is to restore capitalism : a repudiation of Chou Yang's reactionary fallacy adulating the renaissance, the enlightenment, and critical realism of the bourgeoisie.* Peking : Foreign Languages Press, 1971. 45 p.
Translation of: Gu chui zi chan jie ji wen yi jiu shi fu pi zi ben zhu yi. It was originally published in Hongqi, no. 4, 1970.

888.   Yao Wenyuan. *On the counter-revolutionary double-dealer Chou Yang.* Peking : Foreign Languages Press, 1967. 54 p.
It criticizes Zhou Yang who was in charge of the ideological field in China before the Cultural Revolution.

12. Others

889. Bennett. Gordon and Ronald N. Montaperto. *Red Guard : the political biography of Dai Hsiao-ai*. 1st ed. Garden City. NY : Doubleday. 1971. 267 p.
A lively account of the Cultural Revolution as it was experienced by Dai Xiaoai. a student Red Guard in Guangzhou.

890. *Case of Peng Teh-huai, 1959-1968 = Peng Te-huai an chien chuan chi.* Kowloon : Union Research Institute. 1968. 494 p.

891. Chang Hsin-cheng. *Evening chats at Yenshan; or, the case of Teng To.* Berkeley : Center for Chinese Studies. University of California. 1970. 56 p.

892. Domes. Jurgen. *Peng Te-huai : the man and the image.* Stanford. CA : Stanford University Press. 1985. 164 p.
A political biography of Peng Dehuai from his early life to his dismissal in 1959 and imprisonment during the Cultural Revolution. Each period in the life of Peng Dehuai is described within the historical framework of political and socio-economic developments in China.

893. Edmunds. Clifford G. *Bureaucracy, historiography, and ideology in Communist China : the case of Chien Po-tsan.* Thesis. University of Chicago. 1968. 914 leaves.

894. Foster. Leila Merrell. *Nien Cheng : courage in China.* Chicago : Children's Press. 1992. 111 p.
Traces the life of Cheng Nien. the author of *"Life and Death in Shanghai."*

895. Harding. Harry and Melvin Gurtov. *The purge of Lo Jui-ching : the politics of Chinese strategic planning.* Santa Monica. CA : Rand. 1971. 63 p.

896. Lampton. David. *Paths to power : elite mobility in contemporary China.* Ann Arbor. MI : Center for Chinese Studies. University of Michigan. 1989. 379 p.
Contains detailed biographies of six Chinese Communist Party and military leaders: Ji Dengkui. Peng Chong. Gu Mu. Yu Qiuli. Xu Shiyou. and Chen Xilian.

897. Leys, Simon. *Broken images : essays on Chinese culture and politics.* London : Allison & Busby, 1979. 156 p.
      Contents include: Chen Jo-hsi: a literary witness of the Cultural Revolution; Mao Tse-tung and Chinese history; Aspects of Mao Tse-tung (1893-1976); Comrade Chiang Ching.

898. Qin Huailu; William Hinton, ed. *Ninth heaven to ninth hell : the history of a noble Chinese experiment.* New York : Barricade Books, 1995. 665 p.
      Constitutes a life story of Chen Yonggui, who was a farmer from the village of Dazai, became a national model, and in the early 1970s became the vice premier of the State Council.

899. Shambaugh, David L. *The making of a premier : Zhao Zhiyang's provincial career.* Boulder, CO : Westview Press, 1984. 157 p.

900. Ting Wang. *Chairman Hua : leader of the Chinese communists.* St. Lucia, Qld. : University of Queensland Press, 1980. 181 p.
      Simultaneously published: London : C. Hurst, 1980.

901. Yao Wenyuan. *Comments on Tao Chu's two books.* Peking : Foreign Languages Press, 1968. 32 p.
      An article to criticize Tao Zhu, which was originally published on Renmin Ribao in September 1967.

B. MEMOIRS AND FIRSTHAND OBSERVATIONS

902. Barrymaine, Norman. *The time bomb : a veteran journalist assesses today's China from the inside.* New York : Taplinger, 1971. 213 p.
      Detailed account of author's experience in China in the late 1960s.

903. Cao Guanlong. *The attic : memoir of a Chinese landlord's son.* Berkeley : University of California Press, 1996. 245 p.
      In this memoir, the author sketches the tales of growing up in Shanghai during the Cultural Revolution, from the daily life to political upheavals.

904. Chen, Jack. *A year in Upper Felicity : life in a Chinese village during the cultural revolution.* New York : Macmillan, 1973. 383 p.
      A personal account of author's daily life in a Chinese rural village during the Cultural Revolution.

905. Cheng, Nien. *Life and death in Shanghai*. 1st ed. New York : Grove
      Press, 1987, c1986. 547 p.
      Author's own true story of endurance, resistance, and triumphant
      survival over the Cultural Revolution. It painfully documents author's
      persecution in a moving account.

906. Frolic, B. Michael, comp. *Mao's people : sixteen portraits of life in
      revolutionary China*. Cambridge : Harvard University Press, 1989. 278
      p.
      A collection of stories selected from interviews with people moved from
      various places in China and lived in Hong Kong. The coverage is broad,
      from the late 1960s through the mid-1970s and from the South China to
      the North China including urban life, rural life, and in between.

907. Gao Yuan. *Born red : a chronicle of the Cultural Revolution*. Stanford,
      CA : Stanford University Press, 1987. 380 p.
      A personal account of a young teenager in the Cultural Revolution,
      describing Red Guards' activities, relationships between children and
      parents, and other aspects.

908. Gordon, Eric. *Freedom is a world*. London : Hodder & Stoughton, 1971.
      351 p.
      Mostly a chronicle of a British journalist along with his wife and son in
      Beijing during the period of 1967-1969.

909. Grey, Anthony. *Hostage in Peking*. London : Michael Joseph, 1970. 343
      p.
      Records the experience of a British journalist held in solitary
      confinement for two years in China in the early period of the Cultural
      Revolution.

910. Guangming Ribao, comp. *Paragons of Chinese courage : ten who
      braved the storm of the Cultural Revolution*. Gosford, N.S.W. : Lotus
      Publishing House, 1989. 209 p.

911. Harbert, Mary Ann. *Captivity : 44 months in Red China*. London :
      Delacorte Press, 1973. 319 p.
      The author and her sailing companion Jerry McLaughlin were accused
      of trespassing on Chinese waters in the South China Sea. This is an
      account of the author's detention in China between 1968 and 1971.

912. He Liyi, with Claire Anne Chik. *Mr. China's son : a villager's life.* Boulder, CO : Westview Press, 1993. 271 p.
He Liyi lives in Yunnan Province and belongs to one of China's minorities, the Bai. This autobiography records nearly all the major events of China's recent history, including the Cultural Revolution.

913. Ivanov, Ury. *Ten years of my life in the Great Cultural Revolution.* Dandenong, Australia : Dandenong College of TAFE, 1985. 76 p.

914. Jiang Ji-li. *Red scarf girl : a memoir of the Cultural Revolution.* New York : HarperCollins, 1997. 285 p.

915. Li Lu. *Moving the mountain : my life in China from the Cultural Revolution to Tiananmen Square.* London : Macmillan, 1990. 211 p.

916. Li Yan. *Daughters of the red land.* Toronto : Sister Vision, 1995. 319 p.
Records past adventures of the author and her mother and grandmother in China before, during, and after the Cultural Revolution, which paints a personal family drama on a social and political background.

917. Liang Heng and Judith Shapiro. *Son of the Revolution.* 1st ed. New York : Knopf ; Distributed by Random House, 1983. 301 p.
Liang Heng's own story of growing up in the turmoil of the Cultural Revolution as a Red Guard, peasant, and student.

918. Liang Xiaosheng. *Life in Shanghai and Beijing : a memoir of a Chinese writer.* 1st ed. Beijing, China : Foreign Languages Press, 1990. 256 p.

919. Ling Ken; English text prepared by Miriam London and Ta-ling Lee. *Red guard : from schoolboy to "Little General" in Mao's China.* London : MacDonald and Co., 1972. 413 p.
A personal account of a Red Guard from Fujian Province participating in the Cultural Revolution. American ed. published under the title: *The revenge of heaven.*

920. Ling Ken; English text prepared by Miriam London and Ta-ling Lee. *The revenge of heaven : journal of a young Chinese.* New York : Putnam, 1972. 413 p.

921. Liu Zongren; Erik Noyes & James J. Wang ed. *Hard time : thirty months in a Chinese labor camp.* San Francisco : China Books & Periodicals, 1995. 278 p.
An account of Liu Zongren's 30-month internment at the Chadian Labor Reform Farm during the Cultural Revolution. It describes in detail his degrading and dehumanizing experience.

922. Lo, Fulang. *Morning breeze : a true story of China's cultural revolution.* San Francisco : China Books & Periodicals, c1989. 243 p.
An autobiography by a teenage leader of one of the largest Red Guard groups in Sichuan Province, who later became a singer, student, peasant, teacher, and self-taught "barefoot doctor."

923. Lo, Ruth Earnshaw. *In the eye of the typhoon : an American woman in China during the Cultural Revolution.* New York : Da Capo Press, 1987. 289 p.
Reprint. Originally published: New York : Harcourt Brace Jovanovich, c1980.
A story of an American woman, wife of a Chinese professor, in which she tells what happened to her and her family during the Cultural Revolution in Guangzhou.

924. Luo Ziping. *A Generation lost : China under the Cultural Revolution.* New York : H. Holt, c1990. 342 p.

925. Min, Anchee. *Red Azalea.* New York : Pantheon Books, 1994. 306 p.

926. Min, Anchee. *Red azalea : life and love in China.* London : V. Gollancz, 1993. 252 p.
A story of a young woman's emotional and political education during the Cultural Revolution.

927. Ming, Sung and Min Tsu; A. F. Harper, ed. *Never alone : a story of survival under the Gang of Four.* Kansas City, MO : Beacon Hill Press of Kansas City, 1983. 149 p.

928. Milton, David and Nancy Milton. *The wind will not subside : years in revolutionary China, 1964-1969.* New York : Pantheon Books, 1976. 397 p.
Based on what authors learned and saw in China from 1964-1969, when they worked at the Peking First Foreign Languages Institute.

929. Niu-niu. *No tears for Mao : growing up in the Cultural Revolution.*
      Chicago, IL : Academy Chicago Publishers, 1995. 279 p.
      An eyewitness account of the author as a child and her intellectual
      family's suffering during the Cultural Revolution.

930. Rittenberg, Sidney and Amanda Bennett. *The man who stayed behind.*
      New York : Simon and Schuster, 1993. 476 p.
      An eyewitness account of history as it unfolded. Rittenberg went to
      China in the mid-1940s and lived alongside the Chinese revolutionaries.
      He describes his experience in the Cultural Revolution, and offers the
      inside view of power seizure during the Cultural Revolution of a major
      Chinese government body. He also presents a personal story as a political
      prisoner on spy charges in the Cultural Revolution.

931. Rittenberg, Sidney and Amanda Bennett. *The man who stayed behind.*
      New York : Simon and Schuster Audio, 1993. 2 sound cassettes (3
      hours).
      Abridged. Read by Josef Sommer.

932. Ross, James R. (James Rodman). *Caught in a tornado : a Chinese
      American woman survives the Cultural Revolution.* Boston :
      Northeastern University Press, 1994. 175 p.
      A Chinese American women, Wen Zengde's personal story of hope,
      determination, and survival during the Cultural Revolution.

933. Sulzberger, C. L. (Cyrus Leo). *Postscript with a Chinese accent :
      memoirs and diaries, 1972-1973.* New York : Macmillan, 1974. 401 p.

934. Sun-Childers, Jaia and Douglas Childers. *The white-haired girl :
      bittersweet adventures of a little red soldier.* New York : Picador
      USA/St. Martin's Press, 1996. 320 p.
      Records the personal and historic events that shaped the author's life, the
      family, and the country.

935. Thurston, Anne F. *Chinese odyssey : the life and times of a Chinese
      dissident.* New York : Scribner's, 1991. 440 p.

936. Wang Chaotian. *A Red Guard tells his own story.* Taipei : Asian
      Peoples' Anti-Communist League, 1967. 69 p.
      Translation of: Wo shi yi ge hong wei bing.

937. Wang Li; Michael Schoenhals, ed. *An insider's account of the Cultural Revolution : Wang Li's memoirs.* Armonk, NY : M.E. Sharpe, 1994. 96 p.
Memoirs of Wang Li, who was a member of the CCP Central Cultural Revolution Group between 1966 and 1967. It was published as Chinese Law and Government, vol. 27, no. 6.

938. Watt, George. *China 'spy.'* London : Johnson, 1972. 208 p.
A description of the author's suffering in the Cultural Revolution in Lanzhou, China, where he worked as an engineer and was arrested for allegedly spying.

939. Wen Chihua; Bruce Jones, ed. *The red mirror : children of China's Cultural Revolution.* Boulder, CO : Westview Press, 1995. 170 p.
Through the eyes of a child, the author presents stories bringing to life the tragic personal impact of the Cultural Revolution on the families of China's intellectuals during the period of 1965 to 1976.

940. Wong, Jan. *Red China blues : my long march from Mao to now.* Toronto ; New York : Doubleday/Anchor Books, 1996. 405 p.
Records author's experiences in China. She first went to China in 1972 as a Maoist and lived there for six years during the Cultural Revolution. In the late eighties she returned to China as a journalist.

941. Wu, Hongda Harry and Carolyn Wakeman. *Bitter winds : a memoir of my years in China's Gulag.* New York : J. Wiley, 1994. 290 p.
A personal story of Wu's nineteen-year experience in prison and labor camp during the period of 1960-1979.

942. Wu Ningkun. *Single tear : a family's persecution, love, and endurance in Communist China.* 1st paperback ed. Boston : Little, Brown and Co., 1993. 367 p.
The author returned to China in 1951 and served as a professor, but was treated as a counter-revolutionary and an ultrarightist later. It is an account of what the author suffered in the early 1950s through the Cultural Revolution of the late 1960s and 1970s, and into the 1980s.

943. Yan Jiaqi. *Toward a democratic China : the intellectual autobiography of Yan Jiaqi.* Honolulu : University of Hawaii Press, 1992. 285 p.
Translation of: Wo de si xiang zi zhuan.
Records his account of early training in science field, the Cultural Revolution, the Tiananmen Incident of 1976, the Democracy Wall

movement of 1978-79, and the reform in the 1980s. Also describes the momentous events of the spring of 1989, and his life after June 4, 1989.

944.   Yang Jiang. *A cadre school life, six chapters.* Hong Kong : Joint Publishing Co. ; New York : Readers International, 1984. 91 p.
Translation of: Gan xiao liu ji.
A personal description of one woman's attempt to maintain dignity, a sense of humor, and perspective in a trying situation. The author was sent from Beijing to cadre schools in rural Henan in 1970.

945.   Yang Jiang. *Lost in the crowd : a Cultural Revolution memoir.* Melbourne, Australia : McPhee Gribble, 1989. 133 p.
Translation of: Gan xiao liu ji and Bing wu ding wei nian ji shi.

946.   Yang Jiang. *Six chapters from my life "Downunder."* Seattle : University of Washington Press, 1984. 128 p.
Translation of: Gan xiao liu ji.

947.   Yang, Rae. *Spider eaters : a memoir.* Berkeley : University of California Press, 1997. 285 p.
The author joined the Red Guards in Beijing at age fifteen and went to the countryside at seventeen. It incorporates the legends, folklore, and local customs of China to evoke the political and moral crises that the revolution brought upon her over three decades, from 1950 to 1980.

948.   Yang Xiguang and Susan McFadden. *Captive spirits : prisoners of the Cultural Revolution.* Hong Kong ; New York : Oxford University Press, 1997. 302 p.
Translation of: Niu guei she shen lu.

949.   Yue Daiyun; written by Carolyn Wakeman. *To the storm : the odyssey of a revolutionary Chinese woman.* Berkeley : University of California Press, 1985. 405 p.
A story of Yue Daiyun's role as a participant in, and sometimes victim of, China's political campaigns. A detailed description of her often conflicting roles in the revolution as a teacher, scholar, mother, wife, daughter, and friend.

950.   Zhai Zhenhua. *Red flower of China.* New York : Soho, c1992. 245 p.
A personal account by the author who was not only a witness to the Cultural Revolution, but also a participant in it.

951.   Zhang Rong. *Wild swans : three daughters of China.* New York : Simon & Schuster, c1991. 524 p.
       Presents stories to describe the impact of the revolutions on three generations in 20th century China.

952.   Zhang Zhimei. *Foxspirit : a woman in Mao's China.* Montreal, Quebec : Vehicule Press ; East Haven, CT : Distributed in the U.S. by Inland Book Co., 1992. 234 p.

953.   Zhu Xiaodi. *Thirty years in a red house : a memoir of childhood and youth in communist China.* Amherst : University of Massachusetts Press, 1998. 256 p.
       A personal account of a man who grew up in China and witnessed the tumultuous years of the Cultural Revolution. It is as much the story of the author's heroic father as it is of the young author himself.

VII

Travelers' Reports

954. Burchett, Wilfred and Rewi Alley. *China : the quality of life.* New York : Penguin Books, 1976. 312 p.
A report of the authors' travels across China including topics on communes, health care, and minorities.

955. Chiang, Yee. *China revisited : after forty-two years.* New York : Norton, 1977. 180 p.
After an absence of forty-two years, the author returned to China, told of his travel, and recorded his impressions of China.

956. Durdin, Tillman, James Reston and Seymour Topping ; Frank Ching, ed. *Report from Red China.* New York : Quadrangle Books, 1971. 367 p.
Other title: *New York Times report from Red China.*
Stories told by the first American newspaperman to report from China since the Cultural Revolution, by an editor and columnist of the Times, and by a reporter who revisited China after twenty-one years away from there.

957. Fisher, Lois. *A Peking diary : a personal account of modern China.* New York : St. Martin's Press, 1979. 256 p.
Focuses on details of daily life in Beijing covering the period of 1973-1976, when she lived in Beijing with her journalist husband.

958. Fok, Pat and Ross Terrill. *Faces of China : tomorrow, today, yesterday.* London : Michael Joseph, 1974. 190 p.

959. Galbraith, John Kenneth. *A China passage*. Boston : Houghton Mifflin, 1973. 143 p.
A scholar from Harvard presents in the form of a day-to-day account of his three-week visit in China in 1972.

960. Galston, Arthur William and Jean Savage. *Daily life in People's China*. New York : Crowell, 1973. 255 p.
Based on the travel diaries of an American biologist who visited China in 1971 and 1972 living in communes as well as touring cities, universities, and research institutes.

961. Goldwasser, Janet and Stuart Dowty. *Huan-ying : workers' China*. New York : Monthly Review Press, 1975. 404 p.
Based on authors' extensive field notes. Contains detailed records of what they saw in China, what people told them, and what they felt about it at the time.

962. Hsu-Balzer, Eileen, Richard J. Balzer, and Francis L. K. Hsu. *China day by day*. New Haven : Yale University Press, 1974. 111 p.
Authors saw their relatives in China and visited communes, factories, schools, universities, and workers' homes meeting people from all walks of life.

963. Kraft, Joseph. *The Chinese difference*. New York : Saturday Review Press, 1973. 113 p.
The author traveled in China in 1972. He describes the Nanjing Yangtze River bridge, May 7th Cadre School, factories, and communes. He also interviewed some Chinese officials. Half of his book is about Nixon's visit to China.

964. Leys, Simon. *Chinese shadows*. New York : Viking Press, 1977. 220 p.
Based on author's six-month stay in China in 1972.

965. Macciocchi, Maria Antonietta. *Daily life in revolutionary China*. New York : Monthly Review, 1972. 506 p.
The author, a leading member of the Italian Communist Party, took a two-month visit to China in 1970 for the purpose of reporting on life in China.
Translation of: Dalla Cina.

966. McCullough, Colin. *Stranger in China*. New York : Morrow, 1973. 292 p.

Presents a picture of life in Beijing in the period of 1968-1970. The author was working as a correspondent stationed in Beijing along with his wife and daughter.

967. Myrdal, Jan and Gun Kessle. *China : revolution continued.* New York : Pantheon Books, 1971. 224 p.
The authors visited a village in Northern Shaanxi Province in 1969 and interviewed the villagers and reported on the nature of the Cultural Revolution at the local level.

968. Printz, Peggy and Paul Steinle. *Commune : life in rural China.* New York : Dodd, Mead, 1977. 192 p.
A report based on authors' three-week stay in a people's commune in China.

969. Salisbury, Charlotte Y. *China diary.* New York : Walkers, 1973. 210 p.
Records a trip to China from May to July of 1972. The author visited cities including Beijing, Shanghai, Wuhan, Xi'an, Changsha, and Hong Kong, covering countryside and cities, farms and factories, schools and hospitals.

970. Salisbury, Harrison Evans. *To Peking and beyond : a report on the new Asia.* New York : Quadrangle Books, 1977. 308 p.
In 1972, the author spent two weeks visiting North Korea and six weeks in China. He reports on Sino-Soviet relations, the population problem, and other issues. He also describes the interviews with Zhou Enlai, Prince Norodom Sihanouk, and Kim Il-Song.

971. Snow, Edgar. *The long revolution.* New York : Random House, 1972. 269 p.
A report of the author's six-month visit in China in 1970-71. He describes the barefoot doctor, the May 7th cadre schools, acupuncture, marriage, birth control, communes, army, and other aspects, and records interviews with Mao Zedong and Zhou Enlai.

972. Terrill, Ross. *Eight hundred million : the real China.* Boston : Little, Brown, 1972. 235 p.
The author visited China in 1971. He describes the changes since the Cultural Revolution and reports an interview with Zhou Enlai.

973. Terrill, Ross. *Flowers on an iron tree : five cities of China.* Boston : Little, Brown, 1975. 423 p.

A report of author's visit to Shanghai, Dalian, Hangzhou, Wuhan, and Beijing in 1973.

974. Topping, Seymour. *Journey between two Chinas.* New York : Harper, 1972. 459 p.
      The author revisited China in 1974 after an absence of twenty-two years. His trip ended with an interview with Zhou Enlai.

975. Worsley, Peter. *Inside China.* East Ardsley, Wakefield : EP Publishing Limited, 1978. 270 p.
      Based on author's three-week visit to China in 1972 as a professor of sociology.

VIII

Audio-visual and Microform Materials

976. American Consulate General, Hong Kong. *Current background.* Hong Kong : American Consulate General, 1950-1977. no. 1-1,065 (26 microfilm reels).
Consists of translations from Chinese newspapers, magazines, and press releases on major political and economic themes or events.

977. American Consulate General, Hong Kong. *Index to Survey of China mainland press, Selections from China mainland magazines, and Current background.* Hong Kong : American Consulate General, 1960-1977. 15 v. in microfilm reels.
Issues published in 1973-1977 under the title: *Index to Survey of People's Republic of China press, Selections from People's Republic of China magazines, and Current background.*
Three series were brought under bibliographical control by the American Consulate General in Hong Kong through this bimonthly index.

978. American Consulate General, Hong Kong. *Selections from China Mainland magazines.* Hong Kong : American Consulate General, 1960-1977. no. 213-943 in microfilm reels + supplement no. 1-93 in microfilm reels.
Issues published in 1973-1977 under the title: *Selections from People's Republic of China magazines.*
Contains translations of articles from Chinese periodicals.

979.   American Consulate General, Hong Kong. *Survey of China mainland press*. Hong Kong : American Consulate General, 1950-1977. no. 1-6,434 in microfilm reels + supplement no. 1-393 in microfilm reels.
Issues published in 1973-1977 under the title: *Survey of People's Republic of China press*.
Contains translations of Xinhua News Agency press releases, translations of articles and editorials from major newspapers, and the texts of Xinhua News Agency English-language releases.
Superseded in part by: *Daily report : People's Republic of China*, in 1977.

980.   *Art in the Cultural Revolution : establishment of a new age* [Videorecording]. New York : Cinema Guild, 1997. 1 videocassette (33 minutes).
Director Kubert Leung; producers Ping-Jie Zhang and Kubert Leung.
Examines the art policies during the Cultural Revolution through a detailed study of paintings, posters and operas--from their color scheme and their treatment of light and shadow to the bodily poses and facial expressions. It reveals how the Chinese artists were politically mobilized under the guidance of Jiang Qing to promote a revolutionary ideology.

981.   Chao, Jonathan. *A history of the church in China since 1949*. Grand Rapids, MI : Institute of Theological Studies, 1993. 12 sound cassettes + 1 study guide (52 p.).
A series of twenty-four lectures on the history of the Christian church in China, presented by Jonathan Chao. Contents include: The Cultural Revolution and Christian suffering, 1966-1969 (Tape 5); The church under the Gang of Four, 1969-1976 (Tape 6).

982.   *China : a century of revolution* [Videorecording]. [Los Angeles?] : WinStar Home Entertainment, 1997. 3 videocassettes (360 minutes).
Originally broadcasted on PBS. Written, produced, and directed by Sue Williams.
Tells the story of the eight decades of upheavals in China which followed with the 1911 Revolution. Contains interviews with people who participated in the events.
Pt. 1. China in revolution, 1911-1949. Pt. 2. The Mao years, 1949-1976. Pt. 3. Born under the red flag, 1976-1997.

983.   *China : a changing nation : looking at flowers from horseback* [Filmstrip]. New York : Random House, 1974. 4 filmstrips + 4 cassettes.
Authors: Nancy Jervis, Susan Kempler, Doreen Rappaport.

Focuses on many changes that have occurred within the lives of the Chinese people since 1949 in the areas of industry, agriculture, education, health care, art, dance, recreation, and politics.
Pt. 1. Urban life: make the old serve the new. Pt. 2. The great vegetable garden brigade: times have changed. Pt. 3. Industry: unite and take part. Pt. 4, The cultural revolution: serve the people.

984. *China : a network of communes* [Motion picture]. Chicago : Encyclopedia Britannica Educational Corp., 1977. 1 reel (15 minutes).
Edited from the motion picture issued in 1973 under the title: *The awakening giant.*
Shows communes in China engaged in various kinds of production activities. Investigates the Chinese concept of the farm-factory in which communes are encouraged to become self-sufficient and to mass-produce.

985. *China: an open door?* [Videorecording]. Van Nuys, CA : Aims Media, 1986. 3 videocassettes (55 minutes).
Reproduced from a motion picture issued in 1972-1973.
Pt. 1. *An awakening giant,* describes the rise of communism and the revolutionary government in China.
Pt. 2. *The past is prologue,* gives insight into the major internal struggles of China, including the civil war between the Nationalists and the communists, and the role of the Red Guard in the Cultural Revolution.
Pt. 3. *Today and tomorrow,* focuses on the political and cultural image of the country in the early 1970s.

986. *China : the Cultural Revolution* [Videorecording]. Toronto, Ontario : Media Centre, University of Toronto, 1980. 2 videocassettes (60 minutes).
Created by Cecilia Shickman and Hans Pohl.
Using archival photographs, drawings, and posters, this documentary film details the most important events of the Cultural Revolution. Part 1. Preludes, covers events leading to the outbreak of the revolution. Part 2. Convulsions, follows the course of the revolution to its conclusion.

987. *China : the east is red* [Motion picture]. Santa Ana, CA : Doubleday Multimedia, 1971. 1 film reel (20 minutes).
Examines the economic and cultural problems in China. Traces the development of these problems from the social and political traditions of the past.

988. *China : the PBS series* [Videorecording]. New York : Zeitgeist Films,
      1997. 3 videocassettes (360 minutes).
      Originally broadcasted on PBS. Written, produced, and directed by Sue
      Williams. Tells the story of the eight decades of upheavals in China
      which followed with the 1911 Revolution. Contains interviews with
      people who participated in the events.
      Pt. 1. China in revolution. 1911-1949. Pt. 2. The Mao years, 1949-1976.
      Pt. 3. Born under the red flag, 1976-1997.

989. *China, Mao to now* [Videorecording]. Los Angeles, CA : J. Gotoh, 1982.
      1 videocassette (58 minutes).
      Also issued as a motion picture.
      Examines the daily lives of a rural Chinese family living in a commune
      and an urban Chinese family working in a factory. Family members talk
      about how their lives were affected by the Cultural Revolution, and
      discuss the adjustments they have made.

990. *China rising. Vol. 3, Roads to freedom* [Videorecording]. New York :
      History Channel/A&E Home Video, 1996. 1 videocassette (50 minutes).
      Originally broadcasted on the History Channel in 1991. Produced and
      directed by Gwyneth Hughes.
      Part 3 of a three-part history of China in the twentieth century. Describes
      the Cultural Revolution of 1960s & 1970s, and economic reforms of the
      1980s & 1990s.

991. *China's new look* [Filmstrips]. Bedford Hills, NY : Educational
      Enrichment Materials, 1977. 10 filmstrips (567 fr.) + 10 cassettes.
      An introduction to the people, economy, culture, social and political
      institutions, and way of life in China. Contrasts traditional rural styles of
      Chinese living with modern urban life in Beijing.

992. *Chinese revolution* [Videorecording]. Princeton, NJ : Films for the
      Humanities & Sciences, 1993. 1 videocassette (36 minutes).
      Documents the political history of China from the revolution in 1911 to
      the 1989 Tiananmen Square incident. It shows how Mao Zedong and the
      Communist Party began to organize 700 million people into one China;
      China's involvement in the Korean War; the split between Beijing and
      Moscow; the Cultural Revolution; and others.

993. *It's right to rebel* [Videorecording]. Princeton, NJ : Films for the
      Humanities, 1984. 1 videocassette (20 minutes).

Segment from the television program: *History in action*. Producer, director: Julia Spark.

Explains the meaning and results of Mao Zedong's slogan, "It's right to rebel." Discusses the Chinese Cultural Revolution. Includes archival film footage.

994.   *Looking for Mao* [Videorecording]. Boston ; Washington, DC : WGBH Education Foundation; PBS Video, 1983. 1 videocassette (58 minutes).
Tours modern China, illustrating cultural and social changes after Mao. Stresses Mao's continuing influences on China's future. Contrasts the philosophy of the Cultural Revolution with the realities of Chinese life, and compares urban and rural life in China.

995.   Lowy, George, ed. *Documents on contemporary China, 1949-1975 : a research collection*. Greenwich, CT : JAI Press, 1976-1977. 525 microfiches.
Accompanied by a printed guide with same title.
Contents include: Red Guard translations documents; Enactments of party and government documents; Research and analysis reports documents; Leadership information/bibliography/reference documents; Provincial/municipal data documents.

996.   *Mao, organized chaos* [Videorecording]. New York ; Northbrook, IL : Learning Corporation of America, 198-. 1 videocassette (24 minutes).
Originally shown in Canada on the television program entitled: *Portraits of power.*
Points out China's difficulties at home and abroad after 1949. Examines strained relations with the U.S.S.R. and U.S. and shows how the Cultural Revolution brought China into a state of chaos.

997.   *Mao Tse-Tung : the architect of modern China* [Videorecording]. Princeton, NJ : Films for the Humanities & Sciences, 1990. 1 videocassette (30 minutes).
Looks at the life and legacy of Mao Zedong: his early years, the stages of career as a revolutionary leader, the victory over the Nationalists in 1949, the Cultural Revolution, opening to the West, the death of Mao, and the fall of Gang of Four and the Tiananmen Incident.

998.   *Mao years, 1949-1976* [Videorecording]. Boston : WGBH and Ambrica Productions, 1994. 1 videocassette (120 minutes).
It is the Part 2 of: *China, a century of revolution.*

Examines the Chinese modern history beginning from the establishment of the people's republic in 1949 to the death of Mao Zedong in 1976. Reveals the turbulence, famine, violent campaigns, and other major events, including interviews with Communist Party members and ordinary citizens.

999. *Morley Safer's Red China diary* [Videorecording]. New Brunswick, NJ : Phoenix/BFA, 198-. 1 videocassette (54 minutes).
Produced by CBS News, originally issued as motion picture in 1967.
Title on container: *Red China diary with Morley Safer.*

1000. *Night over China* [Videorecording]. Chicago, IL : International Historic Films, 1984. 1 videocassette (45 minutes).
Director and scriptwriter, A. Medvedkin; editor, V. Donskaia.
Edited newsreels of China showing the Great Leap Forward and the Cultural Revolution from the point of view of the Soviet Union.

1001. *One man's revolution : Mao Tse-tung* [Videorecording]. Wilmette, IL : Films Incorporated, 1977. 1 videocassette (20 minutes).
Describes the life of Mao Zedong and his effect on China, covering major historical events including the Long March, the Japanese invasion of China, the establishment of the People's Republic of China, and the Cultural Revolution.

1002. *Red China diary with Morley Safer.* [Motion picture]. CBS News. Released by Bailey Films, 1967. 2 reels (54 minutes).
Documentary of a 21-day visit to China in 1967 by two CBS newsmen, Morley Safer and John Peters. Emphasizes the impact of the Chinese Cultural Revolution. Shows views of five principal cities, including interviews with students, factory workers, and Red Guard members.

1003. *Red dynasty* [Videorecording]. New York : Arts & Entertainment Cable Network, 1989. 1 videocassette (49 minutes).
Writer, Edward Behr ; producer, Peter Firstbrook.
Videocassette release of the 1989 film by BBC.
Covers major events of the People's Republic of China from its founding in 1949 to the death of Mao Zedong in 1976 with eyewitness accounts from university students, teachers, and diplomats who lived during the chaos.

1004. *Salisbury's report on China : the 40th anniversary of the revolution* [Videorecording]. Princeton, NJ : Films for the Humanities, 1989. 3 videocassettes (149 minutes).
Other title: *Salisbury's report on China : the Chinese revolution and beyond.*
Harrison Salisbury is the host of this major series, which covers the history of the Chinese revolution and culminates in the 1989 Tiananmen Square incident.
Pt. 1. *The leaders of the revolution.* Pt. 2. *Slogans and policies.* Pt. 3. *From liberalization to crackdown.*

1005. *Self reliance* [Motion picture]. New York : Distributed by Time-Life Films, 1970. 1 film reel (52 minutes).
Editor Chris Fraser.
Looks at China's goal of industrialization by decentralizing the industry, to encourage local small-size technical enterprises, thereby spreading industrial expertises as well as combating rural under-employment.

1006. *Surviving China's Cultural Revolution* [Sound recording]. Muscatine, IA : Stanley Foundation, 1992. 1 sound cassette (30 minutes).
An interview with Nien Cheng, the author of *Life and death in Shanghai*, by Mary Gray.

Author Index

(All numbers following entries refer to item numbers in the bibliography)

Title Index

(All numbers following entries refer to item numbers in the bibliography)

Subject Index

(All numbers following entries refer to item numbers in the bibliography)

About the Compiler

TONY H. CHANG is Chinese Catalog Librarian and Bibliographer at Washington University in St. Louis.

ISBN 0-313-30905-1

90000>

EAN

9 780313 309052

HARDCOVER BAR CODE